HUMAN
BEING
HUMAN

EMERGING FROM THE ILLUSORY
GRASP OF HERO CULTURE

DEREK STROKON

First published in 2023 by Derek Strokon

© Derek Strokon
The moral rights of the author have been asserted.
This book is a: Derek Strokon - Sacred Line Publication

Author:

    Strokon, Derek

Title:

    Human Being Human: Emerging from the illusory grasp of Hero Culture

ISBN:

    978-1-7390265-47

All rights reserved. No part of this book may be reproduced, stored in a retrieval system, communicated or transmitted in any form or by any means without prior written permission. All enquiries should be made to the author at: *admin@sacredline.ca*

Editor-in-chief: *Derek Strokon*
Cover Design: *Sacred Line Publications*
Cover Photo Credit: *Ray Shum Photography*

Disclaimer: The material in this publication is of the nature of general professional advice, but it is not intended to provide specific guidance for particular circumstances and it should not be relied on as the basis for any decision to take action or not take action on any particular matter which it covers. Readers should obtain individual advice from the author where appropriate, before making any such decision. To the maximum extent permitted by law, the author and publisher disclaim all responsibility and liability to any person, arising directly or indirectly from any person taking or not taking action based on the information in this publication.

Dedication

To you Jenn, my ever-adventurous partner, who keeps me grounded on this wild ride together. I wouldn't want to be doing this with anyone else.

This book is dedicated to the one who when asked, always says "I'm Fine". It's this statement that reinforces the messages in this book, and it's taken me 15 years of you repeating this, to finally understand that, and you have truly shaped me, and have had such a tremendous influence on the belief that I have in contentment, and trusting the process.

You keep me grounded while still encouraging my wild imagination to take flight, keeping me rooted in reality even when my mind is off on its own 'rocket ship' ride. You keep me centered and focused, providing the stability I need to turn my dreams into realities.

But you don't just keep me grounded, you also give me the freedom to soar. You never clip my wings, but instead, provide unwavering support and belief in my endeavors, giving me the confidence to take risks, and explore new horizons. You are my source of strength and empowerment, that propels me forward in my creative and obscure journeys.

You've also given me the courage to stand up for myself. and have taught me the importance of asserting myself advocating for my beliefs. Your unwavering support and guidance have given me the strength to face this life with resilience and conviction.

Your practicality, combined with your quiet strength, keeps me centered and focused, and I'm endlessly grateful for you.

So, here's to you, my understanding, adventurous, and remarkable wife. Thank you for grounding me, letting me fly, and giving me the courage to stand up for myself. I dedicate this book to you with all my heart, knowing that you are the driving force behind my inspiration and creativity.

With all my love,

Derek

Endorsements

"Derek's TEDx was amazing! I was especially moved to tears by his words on healthcare workers and the hero labelling during the pandemic. In "How to Escape Hero Culture: The Power of Just Being Yourself" and "Stop Stalling Start Selling," Derek packs an enormous amount of humour, compassion, and connection into a short amount of page and stage time. I cannot wait for "Human Being Human," and getting to dive into the beauty of resilience and just being yourself."

- Grace Skovgaard
Registered Nurse

"It's amazing how Derek can put his real life experiences on paper and make you feel like you are there in the room with him. His first book, "Stop Stalling, Start Selling" is my go to when I need to stop, refocus and remind myself of how I got to where I am. I can't wait for the shift I'll experience with 'Human Being Human'."

- Steve Lidguard
Advisor, Sun Life

"This book is timely in an era where we have the continued rise of AI and technology. We need to keep our focus on the conversations and moments that matter! Super excited for what Derek is brining to the table in this book. We are truly 'Human Beings'."

- Cadi Jordan
President, CadiJordan.com

"Derek entered my life when I was a young, average advisor, and transformed me into a Convention qualifying producer. His first book shares those teachings and is a book I read twice a year. I'm excited to get my hands on Human Being Human, to keep moving forward with my growth. You don't need to read this book, but you should. When you do, you'll know why."

- Michael Chmilar
Advisor, Sun Life

"Derek Strokon eloquently emphasizes that greatness isn't something you leap into; it's not the hero we see on TV. Instead, being human is all about just being your real self, caring for each other, and living your life, rather than the life others want you to live. Live each day as a human and you'll live your best life."

- Scott Sery
President, Sery Content Development

"By highlighting the human in all of us Derek is able free us from the "hero culture" that shapes modern ideologies. I am excited and looking forward to reading Human being Human by Derek Strokon. The passion for making a difference in this world and supporting others is what Derek is all about. You will love this book!"

- Jacqui Grant - CEO
Break Free Consultancy

Foreword

A number of years ago, I had the pleasure of meeting Derek through a study group known as Pygmalion. In essence, the term "Pygmalion" represents an individual who possesses the remarkable ability to help others undergo a positive transformation, guiding them towards becoming an improved version of themselves. I would confidently assert that Derek perfectly embodies this description. That said, it comes as no surprise that Derek has embarked on writing his second book. Following the publication of "Stop Stalling, Start Selling," Derek made a firm commitment to pursue his literary journey further and when this guy sets his mind to something, you can be confident that he will see it through.

The book you are about to read holds immense value for me as a business consultant, where the focal point of all my interactions is the human as the center of its organization. Throughout my career, I have consistently emphasized the significance of understanding and empowering individuals within organizational contexts. "Human Being Human" perfectly aligns with my core philosophy, which emphasizes the importance of being true to oneself and embracing one's own set of values.

In a world where there is often pressure to conform or follow the hero path, I firmly believe that staying authentic and staying true to our own unique principles is essential for personal and professional fulfillment. Actually, why do we strive to be heroes when the journey of being human is already an extraordinary adventure in itself?

This book reinforces this belief by highlighting the significance of being yourself and embracing your own values as you navigate through life and make decisions.

Derek's perspective and insights resonate deeply with my own experiences and convictions. It acknowledges that each individual is unique, with their own set of values, beliefs, and aspirations. It emphasizes the power and potential that lie within each person's authentic self.

As I read Derek's reflections, I found myself nodding in agreement and reflecting on my own journey of self-discovery. It has reaffirmed my belief that being yourself, with your own set of values, is not only important but also essential for living an authentic and fulfilling life.

Through its pages, "Human Being Human" offers valuable lessons and actionable advice that can be applied in various professional and individual settings. I hope that you, as a reader, will find as much value and inspiration in this book as I have. May it ignite new perspectives, spark transformative ideas, and encourage you to embrace the journey of being a human. Thank you Derek for being... Derek !

- Eric L'Abbée, Professional coach and business consultant

HUMAN BEING HUMAN

Just Be Yourself — 01

Part I

TEDx Surrey — 07
Motivation — 21
Hero Culture — 25
- At Work — 29
   - Athletes — 33
   - Celebrities and Musicians — 35
- Healthcare Workers During COVID — 37
Chaos & Crisis — 39
Tipping Time — 45
Compression — 51
Contentment — 55
Complacency — 59
Resilience — 63
Tying It Together — 67

HUMAN BEING HUMAN

Part II

Relationship Status: It's Complicated	71
It's Not You It's Me	73
We Forgot The Factory Floor	75
Gender - *Kai Scott*	77
Swamped	81
Renewal - *Katy McFee*	83
FOLD	87
WorkHappy - *Greg Kettner*	89
Sacred Line	95
Regression	99
Bottleneck	105
Account-Able - *Ben Burdette*	109
The $10,000 Band-Aid	113
Pizza Over Everything	115
Go Big To Give Big - *Randy Molland*	117
Talking 'Bout A Revolution	123
Disrupt Or Be Disrupted	125

HUMAN BEING HUMAN

On Purpose, For A Purpose - *Luke Askew*	127
Purpose x People x Process = Profit Balance Is Bullshit - *Mike Cameron* Leveraging Technology To Attract, You Must Be Attractive Glamorizing Exhaustion - *Lorna Wilkins* Competence - *Giselle Saati* The Sacred Hierarchy CHO - Chief Heart Officer - *Sandra Crouzet* Drive Safe	131
	135
	141
	145
	151
	155
	159
	163
	169

Continuation

It's Enough To Be Human	173
Every Day Human	177
The Human's Journey	179
Acknowledgements	187
About The Author	189

Just Be Yourself

What if you didn't have to try so hard to be yourself?

How is this even a question? Reading it makes it seem even more ridiculous, doesn't it? Yet almost everybody is still struggling to live a life that is 100% true to themselves. Now by no means am I the perfect example, and although it's long been part of my mindset, I've only really started to focus intentionally on it in the 2 years prior to writing this book.

One thing I do know, is that I want to keep working on it. It's something that we don't spend enough time thinking about or discussing. Our fast paced world continues to gain momentum, and as humans, we are struggling to keep up. Our mental and physical health have never been more fragile, and our disposable approach to consumables, to contentment, to relationships, and how we treat those who entertain us, is challenging the fabric of which we are fighting so hard to keep from tearing.

Human Being Human is a concept whose simplicity can be undervalued and tends to be left ignored. Our ability to provide for ourselves and our loved ones, to live a life of contentment, has been eroding slowly for generations. We have been sacrificing the very thing that we are fighting so dearly to provide for.

The perceived oversimplification of the true purpose of being human has left our current generation seeking more, when in truth the key to living a fulfilled life is to simply, just be yourself...

- So why is it that so many of us have gotten lost in our human journey?
- Why are we addicted to crisis and chaos?
- Why don't we improve our human positions when things are going well?
- What ever happened to the pursuit of happiness and contentment?

I didn't give this topic much regard until a realization was gifted to me by the opportunity hidden inside a significant life shift. I just kind of did what I always did, I worked my butt off, kept my head down, put in the hours, and said Thank You when I was appreciated (which, as is in most cases, happens less often than it should). I didn't realize that I was simply supporting the existing structure. I didn't question why. I didn't know there should be a different way of living life.

We moved to the mountains, and made a strategic life choice to simplify, to downsize our physical and consumable desires, and replace that with the intentional choice of living a life of purpose, on purpose.

Now this may sound like I 'got woke', and if this is how it appears, then you need this book more than anyone. I welcome you to explore this with me, and would love to hear your experience afterwards.

How is it that we have so incorrectly defined who, and how, someone becomes a hero in their own life? We prioritized that becoming an illusory hero, was the primary goal of being human, ignoring the human inside who was struggling to keep up.

We created a life that promotes insatiable lifestyles, making mortgage payments instead of memories, devaluing contentment as the true purpose of being human.

Wow! There's a lot to unpack right there, and I'd like to explore that with you on this journey.

More importantly than solving this problem, I believe that it's important to understand why I feel that this is such an important topic, and why I believe that it deserves more air time. Over recent years, it feels like our society is starting to try to figure out the solution to living, and the solution to modern work. We are seeing a strong shift in focus from the upcoming generation (just as exists in every generational evolution). Priorities are shifting (again), but this time it's different...

As we emerge into a world of unseen before technological advancement, global communication and AI driven opportunity, we are experiencing the greatest shift in the definition of work since the industrial revolution.

Let me make it clear, that I'm all for this! If I can get a computer to eliminate mundane tasks from my regular routine, sign me up. There are those who feel that technology and automation are degrading our human experience, but my opinion is 100% contrary to that. I believe in leveraging the coming technological advancements in order to simplify our lives, allowing us to spend more time being human.

> "It is not that we have a short time to live, but that we waste a lot of it. Life is long enough, and a sufficiently generous amount has been given to us for the highest achievements if it were all well invested. But when it is wasted in heedless luxury and spent on no good activity, we are forced at last by death's final constraint to realize that it has passed away before we knew it was passing. So it is: we are not given a short life but we make it short, and we are not ill-supplied but wasteful of it...
> Life is long if you know how to use it."
> - Lucius Seneca (4BC – 65AD)

For me, the why behind writing this, is about helping us focus on emerging from the grasp of what I refer to as #HeroCulture.

Over the past 50 years, our definition of work, and our focus on climbing the corporate ladder has left far too many people, literally or figuratively, dead or disabled on the sidelines, as the pursuit of wealth (which in most cases is well intentioned – to provide a life of perceived happiness) has gotten us further and further away from contentment. This has been at the terrible sacrifice of our physical and mental health, relationships with others' and relationships with ourselves.

I used to think that I was the only one who saw it this way, until I started to meet people around the world who felt like I did and who were looking to help others change for the better.

My desired outcome for us all, is to be able to take a pause, truly think about our place in the world, and in life. Are we doing enough to focus on ourselves to maintain our health as best as we can? Are we living our lives in tune with what is sacred to us? Are we able to separate the Hero from the Human, and leave the Hero where they belong... On the screen, in the books and on stage?

If this resonates with you, and you want to escape from the illusory grasp of Hero Culture, join us. I'd love to further this discussion. The movement is growing. We call it Every Day Human (www.everydayhuman.me). There are many more of us out there who see a better way. In fact, your life may just depend on it.

It's enough to be human... It's always been enough.

Tedx Surrey

It takes a long time to deliver a 12-minute speech. For anyone who has had the opportunity to deliver a TEDx talk, I know you can relate. In my case, it took me 18 months and to get to the red circle, was some of the most challenging work I've ever done. And what a life changing experience it was.

The team at TEDx Surrey that helped me prepare for this, is one of the finest groups of individuals that I've ever had the pleasure to spend time with - Your selflessness, your passion, your authenticity, and your professionalism are unmatched. Thank You.

I've been on plenty of stages, and I have spoken in front of countless groups over my lifetime, but to date, nothing has yet hit the level of production and passion of the team at TEDx Surrey (www.tedxsurrey.com)

When I was first approached to consider making a contribution and sharing a talk, I thought, "you must have me mistaken for someone else. People like me don't get to do TEDx talks." And to a certain degree, I was right. Someone like me, the way I was, where I was professionally, and my self- perceived worth at the time… that guy definitely didn't deserve to be on the red carpet.

The first time I applied, I was REALLY excited at the prospect of being able to make it to the stage! Admittedly at that point, it was more about the exposure than the message. I made the initial cut, made it as far as the live auditions and top 20. I didn't however make the final 12 who were chosen for the stage.
Looking back, I'm glad it didn't happen that year. I wasn't ready, and I think everyone knew it.

I was offered an opportunity to learn where I had missed the mark, and jumped at the chance to learn.

Life was changing...

This also happened to coincide with an employment shift. I started my new company, wrote my first book, and enlisted the support of an amazing coach to help me re-apply for the next years' talk.

With what I thought originally to be a great platform of self-promotion, has become so much more. It has become my mission in life. It has propelled my self-value, my confidence, and has clarified my purpose beyond anything that I could have imagined.

I believe in myself again – I let myself lose that part of me somewhere along my journey.

Now, we move forward...

I'm including the original Final Script of my talk. They are the words that I had practiced, and although I tried to remember them all and stay on script, they are almost exactly the words that I delivered on the day.

The book that follows is the expansion of my TEDx talk: **How to Escape Hero Culture: The Power of Just Being Yourself.** It is a deeper exploration of what I refer to as Hero Culture and has concepts and recommendations of how to emerge from it.

Onward.

YouTube Title: How to Escape Hero Culture: The Power of Just Being Yourself

Presentation Title: Escaping Hero Culture: What my 2-year-old taught me about being Human

Description: Why are we throwing money at the Global Mental Health crisis, when we have yet to identify the true cause. In his talk, Human Resilience researcher, Derek Strokon, explores the Power of Just Being Yourself, and how we can work back to a life of contentment, emerging from the illusory grasp of Hero Culture. In an honest and authentic, eye-opening talk, that will have you laughing, crying and considering your own journey, he provides a simple solution to a seemingly unsurmountable problem.

Throughline: Our 'Hero Culture Lifestyle' is mentally and physically damaging our Human Journey.

I know... Adorable right?

That's me, the big Spider-Man. The cuter one, that's my son, when he was 2 ½ years-old. We'd just picked up our costumes, and the first thing I did was rush him to grandmas, to show her how awesome we were gonna look on Halloween.

Teaching my son how to be a hero... Living my best life! Spider pose, humungous muscles, ready to take on anything.

Now, while I still agree that it's a super cute photo, I look at it now and I wonder, what was I really teaching my boy?

You see, Halloween didn't go at all as planned. After our epic dress rehearsal the day before, my son refused to put on his costume. He threw it on the ground and said "NO! I don't want to dress up! I'll just be me..."

But why??? I didn't understand! You're supposed to want to wear the costume. We've been training for this for generations! My Dad taught me, his Dad taught him, and there I was, doing what felt natural, showing my son how to be a hero.

After a series of 'failed negotiations', we went out trick-or-treating. Me, head to toe in spandex. The boy, quite pleased with himself, in his jeans and hoodie... It's worth noting that one of us looked really out of place walking through the neighbourhood. (Points at Self) Yeah, it wasn't the kid! I was sure he'd grow out of this ridiculous fantasy of just wanting to be himself.

What he was actually doing, was showing me what it was, to be a **real hero**...

So, how is it that we've been getting it wrong for generations, but my 2-year-old had it figured out? Just be yourself.

I discovered something that I refer to as Hero Culture, that I'd like to share with you.

Ever since the incredible success of the movie Star Wars, there has been a very specific formula that has been followed by script writers, almost exclusively. It's the 'secret sauce' of how to write a box office blockbuster. In brief, your protagonist must face a crisis, fall and hit rock bottom, go through a painful evolution as a prerequisite to greatness. Only then, do they become the hero...

This structure dates back to the Greek tragedies, but since the success of Star Wars, this 'Hero's Journey' formula has been repeated with such frequency, (in movies, stories, social media, everything!) that it has become a blueprint in our psyche, and changed the way we tell stories, and has changed the way that we live.

Think about the last story **you** told. Like cancelling dinner plans with friends at the last minute... The gripping tale we share with anyone who will listen, about who done us wrong at the office, or the explanation we give to the nice officer to justify why going a little over the speed limit, was totally unavoidable.

Social conditioning or indoctrination, call it what you will. We took this captivating formula, designed to teach us life lessons, and made this monumental leap, to a universally accepted idea that we must live this way.

Still, one of the biggest regrets of the dying though is... **"I wish I'd lived my life just being me, not pretending to be something I wasn't"**.

In the business world, we are entrapped by hero culture, where people are praised and promoted, based on their ability to... abandon lunch and weekends, stay late, miss family functions, exhausting both physical and mental health, all in the name of being the company hero.

As a Junior Sales manager, it was made extremely clear to me that 40 hours a week was the minimum, but to get noticed, 60 was expected. As a sales rep on the road at conferences, the unwritten rule was, 'you better be the last to bed, and the first to breakfast'.

We've all had that authoritarian leader. But this isn't simply a failure of leadership - they're just treating us the way they were treated by the people who managed them. This is the failure of a system **destined** to collapse on itself, and this pattern needs to stop!

All the while, every Halloween, I kept working on my son. I kept asking him, don't you want to dress up, and the answer was always the same... "No, I don't want to dress up, I just want to be me".

I still wasn't getting it. Yet these examples are everywhere.

Think of how we praised our Healthcare workers for abandoning their own health during the COVID crisis. As if their jobs weren't enough of a burden, we made posters of them wearing capes and interviewed them on National TV, thinking that that, would make it all worth it, as we left them **slumped over** in the hallways, **broken** and **burnt-out.**

They didn't deserve to be made into a spectacle, they deserved better. They deserved to be cared for as humans and should have been given space to make their physical and mental health the priority.

It's no different in Professional sports. Critics **went after** Olympic Gold Medalist Simone Biles for prioritizing her mental health, rather than sticking to the script of being the Olympic hero.

Defending her decision to step away from competitive gymnastics, she said, "We have to protect our minds and our bodies and not just go out and do what the world wants us to do".

Despite disappointing couch potatoes and corporate sponsors everywhere, who were banking on her to satisfy their need for entertainment, she had the resilience to stay real to herself.

She got it! And she has created a significant shift that has started to change the way we think!

How is it that we have so incorrectly defined who, and how, someone becomes a hero in their own life? We prioritized that becoming an illusory hero, was the primary goal of being human, ignoring the human inside.

We created a life that promotes insatiable lifestyles, making mortgage payments instead of memories, devaluing contentment as the true purpose of being human.

Last summer on family vacation after doing all the planning and packing and organizing to go camping in a trailer for 2 weeks with the kids, my wife had only one specific request. It was that when we got to the Historic Gold-Rush Town of Barkerville, British Columbia, to have one of those sepia tone, olden days family photos taken, to commemorate our trip.

Well, there was no way that I could convince my son to "Dress up, like a Voyageur…"

My now 10 year-old son, had an epic meltdown on main street, in front of everyone… "Dad, I'm NOT wearing a stupid hat with a stupid dead animal on it!"

I held him square by his shoulders, looked him straight in the eye and said "put on the friggin' costume, it's the only thing your mother really wanted on this whole trip. Don't be a disappointment".

He looked **me** straight in my eye, with tears in his, and said, "Why can't I just be me? Why isn't just being me enough?"

Of all the chances I had, it took my son to teach me how to be human.

He's never wanted to be OUR definition of a hero. He's only ever wanted to be himself. Despite my best effort to convince him otherwise, he's had the resilience to stay real to himself, since the beginning.

Trying to live our 90 year **lives** like a script that was written for a 90 minute movie has changed what we expect of ourselves, and what we expect of each other.

Just because we learn this way, doesn't mean that we have to live this way.

It's time we separate the hero from the human, and put the hero back where they belong…on the screen, in the books, and on stage… It's enough to be human… it has always been enough.

Thank You!

Part I

Motivation
Dennis The Dentist

I never intended this to be the first chapter of this book. It felt 'too vulnerable'. I really struggled with how to frame the story about my Dad to get the appropriate message across. Without this as context however, I don't think that it would be half as meaningful as I hope it to be.

I could write this whole book without bringing this up and it would still be effective. But in sharing this story with a number of confidants, it became clear to me that this part of the book is really the most important part of the story. There are countless Mom's and Dad's from the previous generation that are experiencing the same fate.

You see, my Dad has ALWAYS been my hero... I can sense what you're thinking, "yeah, you're supposed to say that".

Well, it's deeper than what it seems.

My Dad is my Hero. He skipped 2 grades in public school, completed his University degree by 19, finished dental school by 22, and opened his practice that same year.

I would confidently say that he and my Mom are more in love now (50+ years married) than they were on their wedding day. He is an amazing husband, father, and grandfather. He ran an incredible business, is a celebrated international speaker, and is published in books and journals around the globe.

And at 65, he crashed... physically and emotionally.

But Wait... HOW DOES A HERO CRASH? It's doesn't go that way. Hero's stay strong. They save the day. They remain infallible. How could this happen to MY dad. The man who raised me and showed me how to be the strong man, loving husband, and Hero to MY kids.

It didn't make sense. I've never read a story or seen a movie with this kind of ending. This must be a mistake.

Over the past 9 years, my fathers mental and physical health has been continually challenged. Without a specific diagnosis, but with the plausible cause of growing up in a generation that never spoke of or dealt with emotional trauma, coupled with a medical system that is overstressed and unable to treat the problem, covers up symptoms with medication, and then adds more medication to cover up the side effects my father has been struggling with.

He (with Mom by his side) has been on a journey that none of us would have expected, nor would a lesser man have had the fortitude to keep pushing through. He has had some incredible challenges that he continues to struggle with.

Motivation

I know that he and Mom have had much more serious talks about how - and whether to, carry on living the way they were forced to, due to his health challenges. If you make a list of undiagnosable physical ailments and medications prescribed to someone going through physical and emotional trauma, my Dad would check almost all the boxes.

I am not putting this into the book to promote a sympathetic response, I am including it because the frequency of this in the baby-boomer generation is far to common place. These stories are everywhere.

Like too many of the baby-boomer generation, my Dad spent so much of his life being the Hero for others', and he sacrificed his own mental and physical health for it along the way. For so many, focusing on contentment, dealing with your childhood trauma, and taking time to talk about your feelings was never even an option. You just soldiered on.

I know that I can't make my Dad better, believe me, I've done everything that I can think of to help. My Dad is still MY Hero. He always will be. He's my example of what it is to be a great man, but he's also a Hero who needed more time to focus on himself and to have the opportunity to escape Hero Culture.

If only he had been afforded the space and support to make his mental health the priority, I believe that this could have changed his situation, and the last 9 years of his life.

He continues to work on himself, and his efforts are now as much for him, as they are for us. He is still my Hero, but he is also now more Human.

My dream is that by having this conversation more openly, that we are able, collectively, to help ourselves and help each other to be human, instead of being required to pretend to be Hero's. I can't change what my Dad is going through, but by creating space for us to open up more, I hope that this journey can be avoided for someone else.

Hero Culture
What the heck does this mean?

With so many buzz words that have been flying around lately, do we really need another one?

I believe that there is an important distinction here. In my opinion, Hero Culture is the greatest causal factor that has contributed to our toxic work culture, and has spilled out into mainstream media, sports, being a celebrity, and the pursuit of insatiable lifestyles.

It is difficult to identify the tipping point, and in reality, the specific event, if it's even possible to identify, matters significantly less, than the importance of our acknowledgement of its existence.

It could be observed as a post WWII phenomenon, when the Army generals moved into management positions in Corporations, the popularization of the television and when without even asking us, it became a member of our family, or a post-industrial revolution event when consumption marketing came to infiltrate our lives.

Under the assumption that the specific causal effect is likely impossible, and truly less important to identify, we will use Joseph Campbell's Hero's Journey and the writing of Star Wars to identify a point of significant change.

The reason that I am choosing this as the point of origin is to avoid the conflict of a suggested global agenda. This would take us off track, and would do nothing to help solve the problem. Now, although Hero Culture existed before, I believe that Star Wars was the tipping point.

In film school, Campbell's Hero's Journey is touted as the 'secret sauce' of how to write a box-office blockbuster. The formula that can be found by a basic internet search describes that in order to be a hero, one must face a crisis, fall and hit rock bottom, go through a painful evolution as a pre-requisite to greatness, only then do they become the hero.

This 'Hero's Journey' formula has been repeated with such frequency, (in movies, stories, social media, everything!) that it has become a blueprint in our psyche, and has changed the way we tell stories, and has changed the way we live.

Now by no means is this intended to be a criticism of Campbell's work. He formulated the best way to tell a story and share a learning in an incredibly powerful way. He simply made a discovery, and put it into words. The fact that it is so effective is to his credit, not his detriment. It's how we exploited this structure for personal gain, that has had such a impact on the way that we tell stories, and has affected the way that we live.

At Work

The most relatable example, and topic that I will spend the most time trying to help solve, is the experience of Hero Culture in the workplace.

> **In the business world, we are entrapped by hero culture. Where people are praised and promoted, based on their ability to… abandon lunch and weekends, stay late, miss family functions, exhausting both physical and mental health, all in the name of being the company hero.**

It's everywhere in business, isn't it? #TheGreatResignation (I think it should be called #TheGreatRealization), toxic work culture, #QuietQuitting/Firing/Hiring. This systemic issue is such an important discussion.

Now, I also submit that I am no expert on affordable housing, income parity, real estate investment sheltering etc etc… There are experts out there who have incredible knowledge about such things, and it's not me. So for the purpose of staying on purpose, we will be discussing merely this sliver, but it is worth noting that yes, this is a complicated discussion that has many moving parts.

The area that I'd like to focus on is the discussion of Hero Culture in the workplace.

.

It is okay to be loyal and committed to your company. It is okay to grind away to achieve something amazing. But in doing so, so often we forget about the most important person, and that's the Human Being performing the Human Doing stuff.

One of my favourite family quotes that I heard over and over, growing up, was

> "Everything in Moderation, Including Moderation"
> – Oscar Wilde.

This means that it's okay to go overboard every once in a while. Embracing this makes it okay to burn the candle at both ends occasionally, just not to the irreversible detriment of your health and relationships.

The Hero Culture danger here is that we do this too often, without regard for our physical and mental health. It becomes an expectation rather than an anomaly. Our bosses expect us to go to the conference all weekend, and be back at the office bright eyed and bushy tailed early Monday morning.

Another practical example of this would be showing up at the office 2 hours early, but also leaving 2 hours before you normally would. What would your boss think? I can almost guarantee that no one would blink an eye about you showing up early, but all eyes would be on you as you sauntered out the door at 3PM, regardless of you having still completed a traditional full days work.

Do you want to do a little test to determine how much Hero Culture mentality exists in your workplace? If you have a traditional salaried Monday to Friday 9-5 job, send an e-mail to your superior on the weekend. The way that they respond to your e-mail may give you a clear indication.

But this isn't simply a failure of leadership - they're just treating us the way they were treated by the people who managed them. This is the failure of a system destined to collapse on itself, and this pattern needs to stop!

For most managers, enabling this type of behaviour is happening unconsciously. We have become conditioned to accept this as the norm. It isn't until we start to realize this, that we can start to think and act differently.

Athletes

There is no greater spectacle than an Olympic Gold Medal pursuit, the World Cup of Soccer, or the Super Bowl. These crowning feats of human performance are the most formidable exhibitions of Hero Culture.

As the viewing public, we sit there glued to the TV, with our snacks and drinks in hand to celebrate the wonder that is LIVE sports.

We set our PVR's, or tune in, just at the right moment to immerse ourselves in the wizardry that we expect to be performed in front of our eyes.

We feast our eyes, concentrated for just enough time to experience the victory and defeat of sport, indifferent to the sacrifice of the individuals who have committed their lives to achieving this goal.

Now, I am not debating the value of human athletic achievement, nor am I suggesting that we interrupt the dreams and goals of these athletes. What I am trying to point out is twofold.

First off, the way that our athletes are portrayed on television promotes the exploitation of Hero Culture.

Secondly, as is starting with concussion protocols and the players movement to ban artificial turf in the NFL, we need to recognize that these athletes are Human first, and Hero second.

The greatest pioneer and early advocate for change, leading the charge in this area, has been Olympic Gold Medalist gymnast, Simone Biles.

Defending her decision to step away from competitive gymnastics, she said, "We have to protect our minds and our bodies and not just go out and do what the world wants us to do".

Despite disappointing couch potatoes and corporate sponsors everywhere, who were banking on her to satisfy their need for entertainment, she had the resilience to stay real to herself.

She got it, and she has caused a ripple effect, that is starting to change the way that we think.

Celebrities and Musicians

No one on this planet is currently more exploited than actors, musicians and happen chance celebrities. The fame and fortune are addictive and far too often lead to untimely deaths and lives lived out of that individuals control.

The desire to be loved, to be immortalized, to be the Hero is shown in no greater example than in those who seek success in these fields, but the list of celebrities who have suffered ill-gotten fates goes on and on.

It is often times far too late to save our beloved celebrities, and to make an example of them here by providing a list is to continue to promote chaos and crisis, devaluing their lives and innocence.

Let's not minimize these humans by suggesting that the pursuit of fame and wealth precludes them from the respect of being treated as humans.

Healthcare Workers During Covid

Should we drill down further with examples that are a little closer to home?

Think of how we praised our Healthcare workers for abandoning their own health during the COVID crisis. As if their jobs weren't enough of a burden, we made posters of them wearing capes and interviewed them on National TV, thinking that that, would make it all worth it, as we left them slumped over in the hallways, broken and burnt-out.

They didn't deserve to be made into a spectacle, they deserved better. They deserved to be cared for as humans and should have been given space to make their physical and mental health the priority.

I feel that we have made our point here. The learning to be taken away here is that Hero Culture has permeated our society and become a blueprint in our psyche. If we do not put in the conscious effort to bring awareness to this, then we will continue down this path, and the further we go, the harder it will be to escape from.

Chaos & Crisis

The initial research question that initially got me down this rabbit hole that became my need to deliver a TEDx talk, has turned into this book, and is the power behind the movement of 'Every Day Human' was:

Why don't we change when things are good?

In 'Stop Staling Start Selling', my first book, Chapter 1 is called 'Climbing downhill to reach the top'. It was originally a Social Media post that got me connected to the amazing crew at TEDx Surrey, which became the script for the first time I auditioned. The next year, I worked with an amazing coach and mentor (Love you Tania!), who helped me prepare for next years' audition. Fortunately, I was selected as a speaker and you can find my talk: **How to Escape Hero Culture: The Power of Just Being Yourself** on You Tube.

The reason to share the above, was that Tania and I started with the question "Why don't we change when things are good?

The outcome of that intensive 10 weeks of work became the foundation for what lies in these pages, but one of the amazing discoveries that we made prior to identifying Joseph Campbell's "Hero's Journey" as the tipping point for where things shifted was, that as a society, we have an addiction to Chaos and Crisis. The dopamine rush that we get from being in crisis is both addictive and unhealthy.

Let's explain this in a story...

My wife and I are in love... Every day I say to her "I love you wife", and she always replies, "yes dear, I love you too". We live a peaceful and wonderful life in the mountains at a Ski resort with some of the best snow the world has to offer. Our kids are great! They behave incredibly well when others are around, and they're mostly good at home with us.

BORING RIGHT???

Although this is a beautiful story, it wouldn't be a very successful movie.

Let's make it more 'interesting'...

I was in a really toxic relationship before meeting my wife. My ex wasn't very nice to me. She took advantage of my kindness. She had a substance abuse problem and played the victim card with me all the time. She said that I was the only good thing in her life (when she was coming off a bender), and then would proceed to berate me for not being wealthy enough. She also had a lot more sex then I did when we were dating... like A LOT!!! It was abusive and it took me a long time to feel like me again.

But then I met my wife, and she is amazing. ... Every day I say to her, "I love you wife" and she always replies, "yes dear, I love you too". We live a peaceful and wonderful life in the mountains at a Ski resort with some of the best snow the world has to offer. Our kids are great! They behave incredibly well when others are around, and they're mostly good at home with us.

Why is it that when we add in the trauma, the drugs, the cheating and the crisis, that the story seems to be 'better'?

The thing of it is, the GOOD part of the story is the part about me being happy and in love!!!

But when you read it without the preamble and the abuse and cheating, the story hardly feels worth listening to. Why do we give the tragic part of the story so much of the credit?

Why is it like this?

Why can't we acknowledge that the 'boring' part of the story, the part where contentment exists is actually the exciting part? We seem to NEED the crisis.

Now I'm not suggesting that we change the way that we write all movies. The drama, thriller, killer, chiller, action filled blockbusters are fun. My son and I recently rented one of those at home, and we watched it 3 times in 48 hours. What an escape from reality!

But we have changed our lives in a manner that we can't make significant shifts without slamming into the wall at 500 MPH. Without that, where's the rush? We have become conditioned to rely on the crisis as the catalyst for change and human advancement.

Examples like this are everywhere:
- We don't eat properly until we get diabetes.
- We don't leave a toxic job or relationship until we are pushed beyond the point of no return
- We don't start living our lives as the person we truly want to be until we realize that our timeline is cut short.
- We show someone how much we really care, until we can't.
- And the list goes on and on...

This unhealthy addiction to chaos and crisis is crippling contentment as the true purpose of being human.

Our enslavement to the endorphin rush, and trying to live our 90 year lives like a script that was written for a 90 minute movie has changed what we expect of ourselves, and what we expect of each other.

Based on this, I am keenly aware that there are people reading this book right now who KNOW in their heart of hearts that a shift for them in a relationship, job, diet or exercise is overdue.

(You're still putting it off, but can't figure out why, right?)

So we forego contentment in exchange for the high that we get from Chaos and Crisis, even though we know that one of the biggest regrets of the dying is to wish that they'd spent more of their life being true to themselves, rather that living a life that they thought others expected of them.

Tipping Time

Is there a solution to all of this? I believe there is, and part of it comes in the visualization of an hourglass.

I touched on this in the first book as a way to set up a deeper discussion, as I knew at the time that this book would be coming to life. So if you just finished the first book, there's a bit of overlap here. If you haven't read it, might I suggest that you go pick up a copy of 'Stop Stalling, Start Selling'. I'm pretty proud of it too. Lol

I digress…

Visualize an hourglass. You can make it as fancy or as simple as you'd like. Picture the grains of sand falling through the neck (that's the skinny part in the middle). Think of every grain of sand as a moment in your life. From further away, or by blurring your eyes, it looks like a steady stream, all of the dots touching each other. Each grain of sand appears to be connected to the one on top and the one below it.

Think of this as watching your life from the perspective of an observer. As the sand flows through, we see the sand collect at the bottom, connected by a stream of events flowing upward through the present, to the future.

But when we look closer, we realize that all the grains of sand are independent of each other. They touch each other, at certain points along their journey, but each grain of sand is its own experience. Although things may look connected, there actually is no direct connection..

So where are we going with this?

As human's we have a psychological need to make patterns out of the events of our lives. It's how we bring order to the chaos. Creating patterns helps us categorize and understand and make sense of things.

This is the second part of understanding why we have an aversion to change. We rely on patterns to help us emerge from slumps, or we assume that 'that's just the way things are'. We believe that the past and the future are connected to each other. But this is not the case.

> **"It's not the chaos that makes us crazy,
> it's the false expectation of it being orderly."**
> – Tania Ehman

The link of past events to future outcomes, controls so many peoples lives. We think that because something existed a certain way in the past, or that something happened right after something else, that there is a causal effect that is occurring.

This is why so many people believe that future outcomes are

out of their control. This is why we get stuck in our self-created patterns. It's why most people don't change, because they have a self-created belief that they can't.

There is an interesting discussion to have about determinism vs free will here, but that is beyond the scope of our discussion. We're already going to go down enough rabbit holes on this journey, and ever since Philosophy 120 in 1996, I have failed to come up with a compelling reason that either of these has to be true. I'm going to use the German word 'Jein' here, that I learned from my friend Kai Scott, that means that both or one or neither are true. Ok, back to the point…

Let's try another experiment… Let's 'tip time' and see what actually exists in the present.

Tipping time is the process of freezing a moment and examining what is actually occurring. It's a way of helping to remind ourselves that the past and the future are connected only by the present. And in the present, nothing is actually happening. This is a mental exercise, not something tangible.

To do this, think of taking our hourglass and tipping it sideways.

What happens?

All the grains of sand stop moving right? The past stays in the lower bulb, the future stays in the top bulb. So what is happening right now? What is happening in the present?

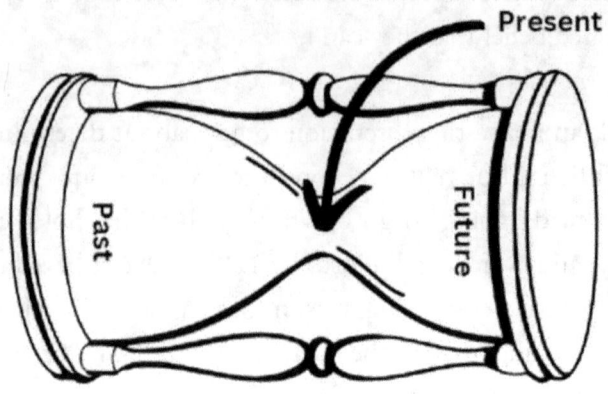

You got it... NOTHING IS HAPPENING!

Let's say that again. RIGHT NOW, NOTHING IS HAPPENING.

And this is an incredibly important understanding. If we had the power to disconnect the past and the future, think of how much more we could accomplish. Think of how quickly we could change!

No longer would we have to wait for things to get better.

No longer would opportunity have passed us by.

There is an incredible amount of power that exists in NOTHING. If we learn not to waste our time, energy and talent, then by truly understanding the Power of Nothing, we can create a reality where opportunity becomes immediate.

The power of nothing allows us to separate past events from future events. Like the eye of a hurricane, the present gifts us with the opportunity of calm, and of quiet.

Our ability to tip time, provides us the freedom to slow down and enjoy the moment. As we will explore shortly, tipping time allows us to truly find contentment. It reveals a space of quiet, a place where nothing is happening. A place where the past and the future do not connect. A place for calm and quiet, where we will find that all the opportunity in the world exists.

This is a very important thing to understand when discussing Hero Culture. When time is tipped, chaos and crisis have no place for existence. Unlinking the past and future, and disassociating events from each other, provides us with an unlimited amount of freedom and opportunity.

When we can truly experience NOTHING, we have the opportunity to find EVERYTHING.

"Write it on your heart

that every day is the best day in the year.

He is rich who owns the day, and no one owns the day

who allows it to be invaded with fret and anxiety.

Finish every day and be done with it.

You have done what you could.

Some blunders and absurdities, no doubt crept in.

Forget them as soon as you can, tomorrow is a new day;

begin it well and serenely, with too high a spirit

to be cumbered with your old nonsense.

This new day is too dear,

with its hopes and invitations,

to waste a moment on the yesterdays."

-Ralph Waldo Emerson

Compression

Let's add a new piece to the puzzle. When things travel through a tighter space than they're used to, they face compression. Sometimes this is helpful, like making diamonds, but many times it just ends up giving you a headache.

Some things can be compressed, and some just crack under pressure. This is the same with events passing through our lives. Just as the hourglass gets narrower in the middle, as does our capacity for processing life events as they creep closer to the present.

When we focus on too many future events, or as the backlog of pending events and challenges builds up, overwhelm can set in. The euphoric experience of our addiction to chaos and crisis, perpetrated by the perverse overaction of Hero Culture life, can make us feel that it's supposed to be that way.

Under normal circumstances, the present is well equipped to handle this flow of events, but if we allow this backlog to build too much, either the events, or the vessel (that's us) breaks.

When we tip time, we reduce compression.

When compression is reduced, our clarity increases, we increase our ability to see opportunity. The time that we have to process information improves.

"Take a breath"

This is exactly what we are talking about when dealing with compression, but in this case, now that we have an understanding of tipping time, and how it relates to Hero Culture, not only does this action increase oxygen flow and reduce heart rate, it also allows us to center ourselves and focus on being in the moment where 'nothing' exists.

Going to 'nothing', where calm and quiet exists, facilitates our ability to rest and recover. It's like putting ice on a swollen ankle. Not only does it make you get off your feet, it reduces the swelling and promotes healing. Natures way of forcing you to slow down.

Something else is also happening here if you can even believe it!

I know...
Have a stretch... Take a breath... Close your eyes for a sec...

See what we did there???

We just experienced nothing together... Did it frustrate you that the page was empty for a bit? If so, head back to the start of the Chapter (Do not pass GO, Do not collect $200).

Ok Ready? Let's Go!

The more quiet that we experience, the more equipped we are to handle an increase in our traffic flow. This doesn't mean that we should take on more, it simply means that we become more efficient, and more equipped to handle the overflow.

This increase in calm, and the power of nothing leads us to a path of contentment.

Contentment

We've worked so hard for an insatiable quality of life. We did it because we didn't know that there was another way. We did it to provide for our family, all the while sacrificing time with those whom we are working so incredibly hard to be with.

In reality, the message from the beginning rings truer than ever. Just be yourself.

Why do we make things so complicated? Killing ourselves to live a life that we thought we wanted, because that's what we saw on TV. Our addiction to Chaos and Crisis, reinforced everywhere we look, continues to promote and normalize Hero Culture.

In the very recent past, things have started to change though. We are speaking more about mental health in the workplace, and people are supporting each other more than they have before. The challenge that I see here is that we have yet to recognize Hero Culture as the true source of the problem, and contentment as the true end goal.

> "You're focusing on the problem. If you focus on the problem, you can't see the solution." Look beyond the problem to see the solution. "See what no one else sees. See what everyone else chooses not to see, out of fear, conformity or laziness. See the whole world anew, each day"!
> -Arthur Mendelson, Patch Adams

In our current world view, contentment isn't sexy. It doesn't have that new car smell. It doesn't have the appeal that matches what we continually see in movies, social media and what is portrayed in advertising. It's doesn't burst in from out of nowhere and disappear just as quickly.

In brief, we see contentment as boring, and boring = bad.

Still, one of the biggest regrets of the dying though is... "I wish I'd lived my life just being me, not pretending to be something I wasn't".

I believe that through all of this discussion so far, the shift in thinking that needs to take place, is to redefine contentment.

Contentment = Happiness ... and Happiness = Good

We've known this all along, but for some reason, contentment became equated with plain. Contentment wasn't the prettiest girl in school. Contentment was simple, and that's not what we learned to pursue.

And this is sad...

Old View: Contentment = Boring = Bad
New View: Contentment = Happiness = Good

I've been wondering where to insert this next section, because it is a crucial distinction that needs to be made. And it feels like it should go right here.

Let's not replace contentment with Complacency...

Complacency

Let's make sure that we don't get caught up in the trap that contentment means giving up, or negating drive. It's not avoiding hustle and ambition (and it's okay if you saw it this way at first – remember, we've been training for this for generations, so the thinking shift may take some time to settle in).

Let's ensure that we don't equate contentment with boring and boring with being complacent.

I'm all for the Hustle, just not all the time.

I'm all for busting your butt. For example, I wrote the first manuscripts for this book in a period of 5 days… 3AM to 8PM, every day for 5 days. I hustled, and I worked my tail off, but I also took breaks and sat in the hot tub, and had naps, and although from the outsiders lens, this looked like a ridiculous goal, I did it.

I've been practicing writing this book in my mind for a long time, I've done my research and interviews, I've batted these ideas around, in deep conversation, and on Social Media, but the actual sit down and write time was 5 days.

I also had a clear grasp of tipping time, and my ability to leverage compression is quite strong right now.

Complacency

So I'm definitely not being complacent. I'm hustling.

Yet still, I'm content. None of this process has come with stress. Pressure? Yes, because I gave myself a deadline, but not stress.

The hustle is good, just not always.

Trading time for work is okay too, as long as you know what you are trading.

Being content doesn't mean that you give up on your dreams. Being content doesn't mean you've settled. Being content means exactly what the French Origin is… To Be Happy!

And this isn't the surface happy. It's not the Happy that we think we see on the faces of the rich and famous. Often times, they are some of the saddest and least fulfilled humans on the planet. This isn't the happy of the CEO, making Millions, on their 4th marriage, and married to their bill payments.

content (v.)

early 15c., "to rest or be satisfied; to give satisfaction to," from Old French *contenter* (from *content* (adj.) "satisfied") and Medieval Latin *contentare*, both from Latin *contentus* "contained; satisfied," past participle of *continere* "to hold together, enclose," from assimilated form of *com* "with, together" (see con-) + *tenere* "to hold" (from PIE root *ten- "to stretch").

Sense connection of "contained" and "satisfied" probably is that the contented person's desires are bound by what he or she already has. Related: Contented; contenting.

content (adj.)

c. 1400, literally "held or contained within limits," hence "having the desire limited to present enjoyments," from Old French *content*, "satisfied," from Latin *contentus* "contained, satisfied," past participle of *continere* "to hold together, enclose," from assimilated form of *com* "with, together" (see con-) + *tenere* "to hold" (from PIE root *ten- "to stretch"). Related: *Contently* (largely superseded by *contentedly*).

content (n.1)

"state of mind which results from satisfaction with present circumstances," 1570s, from content (adj.). Phrase *heart's content* is from 1590s (Shakespeare).

(https://www.etymonline.com/word/content)

Resilience

Could the alliteration have continued??? Could this chapter have been called 'courage'? Well, before I thought about it, these two words potentially could have been interchangeable. Resilience, historically hasn't been the popular choice.
Courage is a 'cool' word. It inspires, it motivates, it makes you feel like anything is possible... in the moment.

Do a quick internet search if you'd like... Over 50,000 books on courage come up instantly, The use of the word has steadily increased since 1980. Interestingly enough though it was on the decline before that, but since the 1500's, it has varied in popularity.

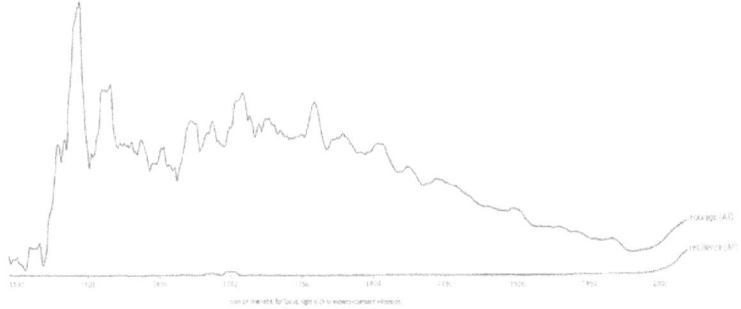

(https://books.google.com/ngrams/graphcontent=resilience%2Ccourage&year_start=1500&year_end=2019&corpus=en2019&smoothing=4&case_insensitive=true)

See that 'other' line? Well, the graph is small and you can barely notice, but there is 'Resilience', trudging along right close to the bottom, staying out of everyone's way, with no need to draw attention to itself.

It didn't even show up until around 1620. It didn't need the spotlight.

But there is a significant difference between these 2 words, (whose popularity seem to be trending very similarly since 1980). Although Resilience lags, it just continues its own journey, happy to be away from all the attention.

Courage is the perfect Hero Culture word. Courage is used by so many called gurus as THE MOST IMPORTANT THING YOU MUST HAVE TO SUCCEED IN LIFE...

News flash Captain Marvelous, You're missing something really important!

<p align="center">resilience (n.)
1620s, "act of rebounding or springing back," often of immaterial things, from Latin <i>resiliens</i>, present participle of <i>resilire</i> "to rebound, recoil," from <i>re-</i> "back" (see re-) + <i>salire</i> "to jump, leap" (see salient (adj.)). Compare result (v.). In physical sciences, the meaning "elasticity, power of returning to original shape after compression, etc." is by 1824. (https://www.etymonline.com/word/resilience)</p>

I like the physical sciences definition, as described above "(the) power of returning to original shape after compression".

It's all starting to come together now isn't it?

Let me be clear, I'm not renouncing or discounting the word courage. It's powerful, and is to be called upon in crucial times. Courage helps us take the leap. Courage stands on the shoulders of resilience and says "okay, let's do it now".

Courage is important, but it is not what gives us the strength to continue on in a state of contentment.

This is where resilience trumps courage.

The greater the adversity, the more we depend on resilience. In the face of adversity, it is our level of resilience that has the longest term impact. Resilience is what gives us strength to be courageous again and again.

Resilience is driven by purpose. Courage is driven by crisis. Courage is a moment; resilience is a movement towards continual mindfulness.

"Courage, it couldn't come at a worse time"
– Gord Downey

Replace the mediocrity of compression with

the power of mindfulness.

Compression is to be used for healing, not to

escape from the reality of our lives.

To have the ability to sit quiet, in the moment of compression,

is where all the potential energy exists.

Right now nothing is happening...

So many people believe that they do not have a choice,

and this is not the case.

Trying It Together

I hope that this is coming together in the way that it was intended. We have just unpacked generations' worth of complexity into small bite size pieces, and I want to acknowledge that it's a lot.

We've made some assumptions and avoided some of the complexities in the real world that affect its immediate application. I have spent a significant amount of time challenging the reality of what I've just written, and it flows for me, but this may bring up some uncomfortable feelings.

I've maintained a level of vulnerability and honesty in these pages that continues to push my limits. I will always keep driving forward in this regard. These pages are the collection of my lived experience, my research and conversations. Have I nailed it perfectly? Who knows. But what I do know is that I want us to keep having this conversation over and over again until we do.

I want to keep exploring this because the way that we are living needs to improve. However this world works, we need to increase the frequency of the discussions that we are having about supporting each other and helping one another heal.

There is a lot of complexity behind the simplicity of 'just be yourself'. Our society pulls us away from this, and our disposable, single use, immediate gratification lifestyles add to this.

When you layer in the complexities of changing the way we work, especially if you belong to a large corporation that is finding it hard to understand where to change first, and understands that change is needed, but is questioning the profitability in the short term, I want to say that I get it.

It's not an easy task, but if this book can save your Mom or Dad, your friend, or even save your own life from the illusory grasp of Hero Culture, then that's a check mark in the win column.

In Part II, we will continue to explore this, and although I understand that it will not be exhaustive, it will add some additional perspective and help get us on the way towards Human Being Human in our working lives.

The reason that we are focusing more on the workplace in Part II is that it is the most common link for us as humans. It is also where we spend the majority of our time for the majority of our adult lives.

Part II

Relationship Status: It's Complicated.

Plain and simple, this isn't easy to navigate. The world that we live in is complex, and the systems and processes that we live with, have been established through decades upon decades of social influence. This is just part of what makes implementing drastic and sweeping change more challenging.

We have been adding layer upon layer onto the complexities of work for generations. With businesses leveraging globalization and scaling up to leverage economies of scale, it is impossible to just come in and make a sharp right, let alone a U-turn.

I used to comment about the global company that I worked for and state that the organization was like an icebreaker ship. The company didn't make hairpin turns, but still forged on as a leader and never stopped pushing forward. When you get that big, nimble isn't always possible.

It's difficult to pivot. Even more, it's even more challenging when you're not 100% sure where to go, or why you're turning.

Another strong analogy here is that these changes are much like driving a car by only using the rear-view mirror.

We know exactly where we've been, and know why we ended up in the ditch last time, but there is no promise of what's coming up.

Even if we knew exactly where we wanted to go, it would be impossible to hop into a magic box, push a button, end up right where we were hoping to. It's too complex. I have friends who have been working on sweeping change for decades and are still finding it a challenge to make in-roads with large corporations.

My great friend Luke Askew pointed out to me in a recent conversation, that the next people joining the boards of directors (yes it's the millennials), don't think the same way, don't value the same things and don't want the same lives. We'll get more into the specifically later, but the point to be made here is that change needs to happen.

As we know, these changes are not going to occur overnight. They are going to occur one small piece at a time, but the more frequently that we have this discussion, the quicker that we will be able to move towards a more Human work environment.

Let's continue, we'll loop back to this in a bit.

It's not you, it's me!

The blame game never gets us anywhere. We all know this, but we sure don't live it as well as we could. Blaming the previous generation, doesn't change the past. Criticizing the up and comers serves absolutely no purpose. We're just at where we're at.

Our desire to blame the other side for what we see as incorrect is not the way to move forward.

What we need to do is to take inventory of where we're at, understand where we've been, and set a new path to move forward.

Those who designed the system, did so, utilizing the information that was available to them at the time. It's that simple. We are but a collection of the experiences that we live and observe.

Blaming the Boomers for building companies the way they did, or accusing Millenials of lacking work-ethic because they have different priorities gets us nowhere.

In order for us to emerge from Hero Culture is going to take equal effort from all camps. We must admit that, "Yup, we missed the mark at certain times, but we can do better".

We must also acknowledge that without the efforts and infrastructure that were put in place before, we would not be seeing this technological evolution that is making the pursuit of this alternate way of future existence a reality.

We forgot the factory floor

To the detriment of too many, I believe that too frequently, we lost track of the role of the manager in exchange for the title of the manager. In the old factory days, the role of the manager was to spend time on the factory floor, engaging with the factory workers to determine what it was the workers needed, to be more effective. They were then to bring this information forward to senior leadership in order to implement strategies to increase efficiency and improve operational flow.

Over the past 50 years however, becoming a manager, became more of a status symbol than a position of servitude. Do this because I'm your manager, and I said so.

How wrong. How horribly wrong. We've all had that authoritarian leader, but they are not solely to blame. We all got here together, and it will take all of us to get out of it.

For the most part, they didn't know any better.

The status symbol of management, being the white collared middle manager has been fantasized and sexualized for decades in film and TV. The ability to control power, to be able to cause or end chaos, and to be the only one to be able to solve a crisis gave being a manager a certain glorified mystique.

Whether reinforced by the army generals with undiagnosed PTSD, or those with low self-esteem seeking approval having never felt love from their emotionally detached parents, management became a platform to abuse others, rather than own the responsibility to care for those in their charge.

This reinforces toxicity. As my amazing and brilliant friend, Jill Moore says "The toxic is exponential, when hurt people lead hurt people".

Our acknowledgement here is twofold.

First, that this is not any isolated incident. It occurs everywhere, and although traumatizing many and contributing to toxic culture, our priority here is to acknowledge this and provide forgiveness, rather than seek retribution, so that we can establish a baseline upon which to implement change.

Secondly, imagine if these individuals had access to the facilities that they needed to deal with their emotional trauma. Imagine if they had a keen awareness of Hero Culture. Imagine how different work may have been for so many of us.

Gender

Kai Scott is one of the most authentic, genuine men that I have had the pleasure of becoming friends with. Go find his TEDx talk called 'The surprisingly Simple Way to Transcend Differences About Gender'. Your eyes and your heart will open.

I have struggled with many of the DE&I workshops that I have attended in the past, as many of them felt to me like soapboxes used by other employee's to further their careers.

Some programs felt dismissive and divisive, touting one community as different or separate from the other. In addition, some of these discussions felt like they were simply a platform for individuals to promote how 'diverse and inclusive' they were by name dropping every trans, or gay human that they knew, to gain approval, neglecting the conversation all together.

Kai is a consultant on gender diversity in the workplace, and his perspective and understanding on these issues is one that brings people together, for the sake of conversation and improvement.

Remember the discussion of 'Jein' from earlier in the book?

In his own words, Kai shares some thoughts on how we can move forward together as Humans, rather than separate as part of different camps.

"There is quite a lot of disagreement about gender between the generations. Many Boomers see gender as straightforward (i.e., men and women as defined mostly by anatomy), whereas Millennials experience and express gender along a spectrum based on what is felt on the inside. While there is nothing wrong with disagreement (as a valuable way to learn from one another), when our discussions become heated, dismissive, and hateful we lose the plot and each other.

Each generation has valid points and is also part of the problem. Many people in the Boomer generation feel overwhelmed and confused by all the new terms and concepts. Some feel inclined to reject it all as pure make believe. On the other hand, Millennials are frustrated by the slow pace of change and point to their elders as the anchors in the mud preventing important forward progress. Neither viewpoint gets us anywhere close to where we need to go. Simply put, both sides are right and wrong at the same time. How can that be?!

Boomers:
- Get right: Created the systems and practices that got us to this point. And good news: They work for most people - hooray! Thank you for laying a solid foundation.

- Miss the mark: The current set-up does not take into account all genders, especially those that are beyond men and women. Boomers also blame and ridicule Millennials for being out of touch with reality.

Millennials:
- Get right: Actively work towards making the world a better place for all people, especially those who have been inadvertently left out.

- Miss the mark: Blame and ridicule Boomers for not knowing about gender diversity and being out of touch with the present. Millennials primarily consider the needs of people who do not fit the mold, without ensuring whether or not changes continue to work for the majority.

Notice that blame and ridicule show up for both Boomers and Millennials. They are a perfect mirror of one another. Who will be bold enough to break the cycle?

The answer: Anyone who can truly listen to one another without needing to change the other. When we do this, we begin to realize that we are saying similar things in different ways. Language is messy – it will likely fail us. But we can find our way back to each other in ongoing, considerate dialogue by maintaining an honest and empathetic curiosity. We may be pleasantly surprised by what we discover and co-create together when we lay down our defenses.

Even within earnest discussion, it can still be difficult. When things get tough, it's ok for Boomers to say:
- "I don't understand. Can you explain it to me (again)?"

- "I appreciate it is important to you that I understand. But I don't have the capacity to learn this information right now. Let's try again in a few hours or days."
- "This new approach will make it more difficult for me and others. What if we tried it this other way?"

When things get tough, it's ok for Millennials to say:
- "What options can we create together so everyone's needs can be addressed?"
- "I don't have the energy to explain this to you right now. Let's try again in a few hours or days."
- "I understand how this new approach does not work for you. Let me take some time to think about the alternative you proposed."

With this type of openness, we can combine the best of both generations, to honour the past and walk boldly into the future."

By Kai Scott – President, www.TransFocus.ca
Vancouver, BC, Canada

Swamped

We have become professionals at being busy.

If you don't want to be interrupted by someone at the office, just increase your speed, and stare at your phone as you walk down the hallway. It works every time!

Being busy has also been something historically that has created a false sense of status. Our addiction to chaos and crisis has created a perspective that busy = success.

But what if quiet = success instead? What if when we were swamped, we just got out of the swamp and found more stable ground?

This world of quiet (ie: tipping time and being in 'nothing') doesn't work in Hero Culture. When we acknowledge the power of nothing and move forward embodying these principles, quiet begins to replace chaos and crisis, the journey towards contentment starts to become more clear.

Renewal

Katy McFee is one of the most inspiring women that I have had the pleasure of getting to know through this new pursuit of focusing on being human. She has reclaimed her life. Her natural ability to comfort and motivate and empower others to choose self and combine it with success is truly amazing.
The thing is, so many people are living the same way that Katy and I did. Rise and Grind! But never rest. Addicted to the work, leaving a path of self-destruction along the way.

In her own words, this is her story... One all too common, rooted in Hero Culture.

"It took a burnout event for me to realize how much I attached my self-worth to my work.

Not to say it was a total surprise, because for years I sacrificed relationships, self-care and any semblance of a healthy balance for career growth. Constant travel, missing kids' events, checking my email during dinner, drinking wine every evening to de-stress...

I knew it wasn't healthy, but I loved the feeling of being 'successful'.

One day I totaled my car on the highway on the way to work. The first thing I did, sitting in a smashed-up Audi in total shock on the side of the highway, was to email my boss (our CEO) to let him know I'd be missing the management meeting and to ensure that he brought up a few key topics that I needed resolved.

Still, it was another 3 years before I fully burnt out. And if you haven't experienced burn-out, it's not something you can cure with a week's vacation in Mexico. I was negative and emotionally fragile. I was breaking down almost daily. I was paralyzed with overwhelm. This was NOT me.

I had built a 'perfect' life with an amazing career. Heck, I had my fancy EVP, Sales title - this is all I ever wanted! And I was miserable.

I knew I needed to make a change because I couldn't ignore it anymore…

I made the decision that I could no longer continue on the path I was on if I wanted to live a happy life…

But even in the face of this, the thought of leaving my job terrified me…

What would people think if I was no longer an exec?

Would I matter anymore? Would I still be important or significant?

And this realization was the beginning of my ultimate shift away from focusing on work and instead focusing on myself. Staring these questions in the face and asking myself who I really was without my title?

The change was not overnight. First, I attended a 2-day masterclass about finding your aligned path. Then I enrolled in a 3-month, weekly intensive coaching program to try and unpack everything I was figuring out and decide what exactly I was going to do with my life.

By this time, I had given notice to my company and was down to 3 days a week while I transitioned out over my last quarter to ensure they were set up for success.

Initially, I thought I would start a sales & strategy consulting business to put all of the great knowledge I had to use, but without a full-time exec job. So basically: same stuff, more balance.

But as I started down my path, I started to uncover a whole host of neglected passions that once on the surface, I couldn't ignore. My passion for writing and creating. My passion for empowering women and helping them create the lives of their dreams. My passion for advocating balance and boundaries so people wouldn't end up in the place I was in.

Maybe most of all, a newfound purpose to show up as the most authentic version of myself in every area of my life.

My life today looks very different than it did 2 years ago. I start every day with yoga and meditation. I block off lunch every day for a solid meal and a walk outdoors. I wrap it up at 4pm... because I can.

I block off weeks of vacation to spend with my family, my partner or a friend.

I now invest in myself first, and work is simply one element of who I am, instead of everything I am.

I'm hugely passionate about what I do. But I'm even more in love with myself and my life."

Katy McFee, Founder – Insights to Action
Ottawa, ON, Canada

Fold

The 'Fear of Leaving Your Desk'. I bet you never thought about it, but it's too real of a thing for so many. If you're reading this book at the office, "Get back to work! You're on Company time!" (kidding – do whatever you want). But seriously, if you're sitting at your desk right now, or next time you are, get up and go for a 30 minute walk... you can even take your phone with you (but if you're really brave, leave it at the office).

OK, Go!

If the thought of this makes you anxious, then you suffer from FOLD.

FOLD is something that I struggled with as an employee, but something that I carried with me into business ownership. We chose to live in a mountain resort town, and we have amazing beautiful trails steps from our front door. It's super convenient to go for a walk, but I hesitated doing this for so long. Even running my own business, this was an incredibly difficult thing to do.

If you practice, it gets easier.

The health and productivity benefits of going for a walk are well documented, but let's think about the Hero Culture response.

Imagine… You're downtown New York City… And EVERYONE just gets up and goes for a 30 minute walk. Holy! Aside from the fact that we'd all be standing shoulder to shoulder and probably wouldn't be able to navigate anywhere, let's just take a snapshot… The Hero Culture knee jerk reaction is, 'look at all that lost productivity'.

Okay… even typing this is making me claustrophobic. Let's spread out a bit.

Go to your work environment wherever it may be. Downtown Toronto, a smaller suburb city of 100,000, small town or work from home remote location.

If you're okay with it, even take off your shoes and socks (Go research the benefits of Earthing – it's brilliant).

What's the worst that can happen? If you can't leave your desk randomly for 30 minutes, even if you have a job where operationally it is crucial for you to be there, then we have a breakdown in our system or process.

Pause is required. Taking a break brings us back to quiet. You might just run into someone who is doing the same, and that may lead to something wonderful.

WorkHappy

Work happy... that sounds simple, doesn't it?

So why when we read this, does it make us light up inside, often followed by the 'well, it's not that simple'. Greg Kettner and I have known each other for 15 years. We first met when he volunteered to help with a Movember fundraiser to support Cancer treatment research and mental health advocacy.

Little did either of us know that over a decade later, Greg would be leading the charge to support, and be positively impacting mental health in the workplace.

His company, WorkHappy, has helped thousands upon thousands of people talk openly about mental heath in the workplace and in their lives. The most valuable part of Greg's work doesn't happen on stage. It happens after, in the hallways, connecting 1:1 with humans to talk about their challenges, and providing them a safe space to just be themselves.

In his own words, here is Greg's story of WorkHappy.

"WorkHappy started because after 27 years in sales and leadership in various roles in the National Hockey League, Major League Soccer, SAP and BuildDirect I was tired of going into work, and doing everything for someone else, and rarely getting the thanks and gratitude that we all desire.

I was just tired of going to work and not being happy. My productivity started to suffer, sales declined and at times, my mental and physical health suffered. I enjoyed my colleagues, but at some of the organizations, the culture was lacking, people weren't a focus of the culture.

Three weeks into Covid-19, my 'manager' told me on a phone call that I was no longer essential, which really chapped my hide. No emotion, no explanation. I thought he was joking. Why had he eliminated my position when I had turned the ship around, increased membership by 140%, increased revenue?

All of a sudden I was without a job. And some manager who didn't know how to communicate with his team or customers was telling me that I was non-essential.

There had to be a better way to work. One where people are valued more than profits. Research turned up few options, so I turned to people I trusted, managers I loved working for like Jordan Thorsteinson and Kurt Comer, they always put people first, so everyone could WorkHappy and prosper.

After a quick conversation with my wife to let her know that my position had been eliminated, I went golfing to get rid of the frustration and figure out what I was going to do to support my family.

I thought to myself, "when was the happiest at work I've ever been?", and that was on a stage doing stand-up comedy and working with my idols like Norm Macdonald and Robin Williams.

Problem is, when you want a great marriage and support your family, 300 nights on the road working for $100 a show wasn't going to work.

And after several conversations with my wife Beck, she said to me, "What about this? You love being in front of people on a stage and making them laugh. You love sales and being around people, and you are one of the most positive people I know. Why don't you share with organizations how to WorkHappy?"

The light bulb moment. That's it. Help others WorkHappy, serve others which would make me WorkHappy.

When people are happy at work they are more productive, they stay with their company longer, and they have better mental and physical health. In fact, happy sales reps sell 37% more than unhappy reps. People who are happy are up to 20% more productive at work.

Also, two years prior, my stepdaughter Rachel, lost her father to suicide. I started learning, researching and taking classes to find out how to help my family and myself through this traumatic experience and found that very few organizations were talking about mental health at work.

I formed WorkHappy to help leaders and organizations reduce turnover, motivate their teams to be more productive, and how to normalize mental health conversations in the workplace and at home.

Finally, I found my passion and purpose, to help others, make difference in other peoples lives while supporting my family.

Every day I have conversations with amazing people and leaders, and organizations bring me into their world to speak, train and coach how to have a WorkHappy culture.

When we put people before profits, everyone wins, including the shareholders.

Why not have more companies with a WorkHappy mentality where employees want to show up, win together and be on a team where they know, like, and trust their co-workers.

Since creating WorkHappy I have met and reconnected with some amazing people like the author of this book Derek Strokon, Geoff Maclaughlin, Jason Wange, Chuck Thuss, Jordan Thorsteinson and Kurt Comer.

When we WorkHappy and have conversations about our mental health, our families, our kids and our jobs, the world is a much better place."

Greg Kettner – Founder, WorkHappy
Walla Walla, WA, USA

One day, you woke up in the middle of someone else's dream.

TEDx Sketchpad notes, Summer 2022

Sacred Line

What do you stand for?
What is Sacred to you?
What are your non-negotiables?

These are 3 of my favourite questions. They are questions that I believe we all need to take more time to consider. We kind of just get caught up in life don't we? I was just looking back at some photo memories from 10 years ago and thought to myself, wow, how did something that feels like it just happened, actually happen 10 years ago.

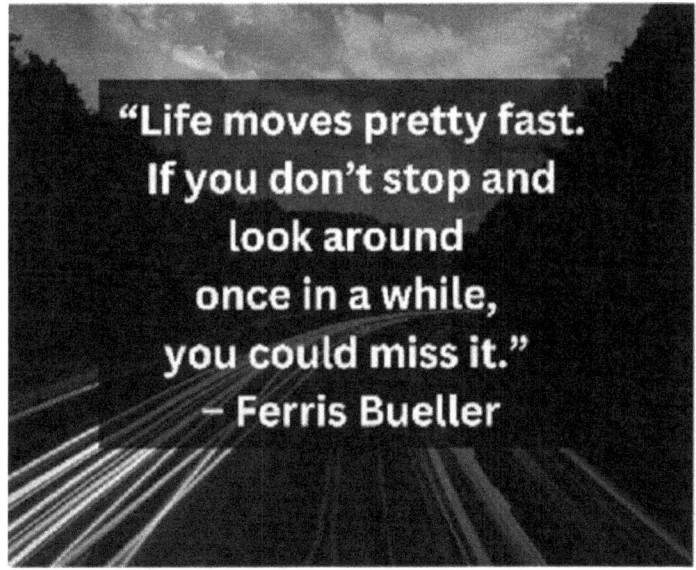

Most people feel that they know what is important to them, but how many people can say with precise clarity what is Sacred to them?

When I started Sacred Line Consulting, even my Mom said, "Using the word Sacred in a company name is a bit too much". And I respect that, because yeah, it was a bold choice.

But what are we if we're not bold? Now, let's not confuse bold with bragging or bravado. Bold is about being 100% unapologetically you. Remember? Just be yourself.

Think of it like this... If you had a theme song that played every time that you walked into a room, what would the words of the Chorus be? What is your anthem? What do you stand for?

This is an exercise that I revisit frequently. What are the 15 words or less that represent you as a Human? I would highly recommend this exercise to everyone reading this book right now.

Think of the words that really resonate with you. What are the words that you remember from childhood, High School or University that stick with you today?

Start a document and write them down. Make a collection, do an internet search, use a thesaurus, do whatever feels natural to you.

Start to string these words together into a sentence or poem or message. However you want to do it... It's your song.

This is not a one and done exercise. It can seem silly, it can feel awkward, it can be liberating.

Once you have a genuine belief in the honesty and integrity of your Sacred Line, you will notice that you will naturally be drawn to align your life with this statement. Your actions and decisions (See: Stop Stalling Start Selling for the chapter on De-Cide to understand the power of a decision) must align with your Sacred Line. If something doesn't match, one of the two things needs to be refined. There will be one-offs, but if a pattern emerges, a correction must be made.

You will start to look at the world through the eyes of what is non-negotiable. You will start to question the validity of things that don't fit.

Coming up with your Sacred Line is not the easiest thing to do, it often doesn't feel like it should be the first step, but it is one of the most crucial steps to take on the Human Journey.

Sacred Line

Would you tell me, please,
which way I ought to go from here?' [asked Alice.]

'That depends a good deal on where you want to get to,'
said the [Chesire] Cat.

'I don't much care where—' said Alice.

'Then it doesn't matter which way you go,' said the Cat.

'—so long as I get somewhere,'
Alice added as an explanation.

'Oh, you're sure to do that,' said the Cat,
'if you only walk long enough.'

-Alice in Wonderland

Regression

WFH, RTO, WTF!

COVID.... Ughhh, can we please stop talking about it? Well, sorry, no we can't, not just yet.

I believe that the lessons garnered from the COVID crisis will continue to trickle in over the coming years. This shared global experience will leave marks on our society for so many reasons, good and bad. The effects of the Global Pandemic have forever changed the landscape upon which we move forward.

March 2020 – Lockdown. The whole world hunkered down under a Global stay-in-place order. Regardless of the outcome, the source, the way you feel now – That was a frightening time.

For the point of this discussion, we will be focusing solely on the 'Work-From-Home' and 'Return-To-Office' part of the conversation.

COVID taught us that most of us don't need to be at the office. Very quickly, we adapted to a work-from-home lifestyle. As the old saying goes,

> **There is no greater motivator than necessity.**

We learned how to build relationships with colleagues and clients in a virtual environment. We instantly got comfortable with virtual meetings, and despite a few cat face filters and wardrobe malfunctions, for the most part, we got it right. And we got it right quite quickly.

Companies that had been averse to adopting e-signature software, citing the regulatory environment, instantly found ways through the red tape that had previously been a convenient explanation to avoid change. And we all know how expensive change is in the short term.

Working from home reconnected us to our families and loved ones, provided us with opportunities to consider our mental and physical health, and gave us the freedom to function from anywhere.

Did we still need to measure results based on time? Or was there something bigger at play? What if the old way of measuring time over results was due for a performance review?
It was very interesting to think about how the future of work was going to show up after COVID. Could this be the shift we needed to escape the hours long commutes endured by workers who chose not to, or who couldn't afford to live in the City they worked in, due to skyrocketing real estate prices?
In 2022, as we started to emerge from being held hostage by a

pandemic, companies started to implement return-to-office mandates. The explanation was that they needed to get their corporate culture back. Workers need to be back in the office!

But is this the real reason?

How do we measure time-based results, if we can't track time? If your staff isn't in the office, how do we know what they're doing?

As was my case, what if they're out for a ski with their kids? Wasting company time!!! Don't get caught up in special projects, like helping out at your kids gym class. That's not YOUR time to spend, 'cus we own your time.

Jody Thompson, Author of 'Why work sucks and how to fix it' (If you haven't read it, read it next) brought forward the idea of ROWE: a Results Only Work Environment. I implemented it in one of the businesses I was managing, and we rose from 86th to 7th in Corporate ranking in 2 years.

What if we measured results instead of time? What if the company just let you go and live your life, as long as you got the results?

My team was afforded 100% autonomy over their time. Want a 2-hour lunch? Go. Done your tasks? Go. Don't feel like working? No problem!

Stay home for as long as you want, turn it into another week off, who cares, just make sure that we get our jobs done, even if that means having someone else do it, as long as the pendulum swings both ways.

This strategy takes a significant amount of trust in your people, and although this shouldn't even have to be said, if you 'hire slow, fire fast' and have the right team (we called ourselves the dream team), trust is not a discussion you need to have once you're through the first interview.

Next, change what you measure! Stop measuring time, start measuring results. It's that simple.

Now I'm not suggesting that a fully remote, location agnostic business model is the way. Nor am I promoting the idea that we should all go back to the office. The answer is - it depends. Find the best way to get the best results in the shortest amount of time and work towards that!

This conversation needs to be had with more attention than we are currently giving it.

Now, in the short term, overturning a complete business model, regardless of the project or reason, is admittedly very costly in the short term.

The logistics, especially with multi-national corporations, is a nightmare for those doing the operational implementation.

The short term expense is significant both on the income, and cost of implementation side.

But I do believe that this conversation needs to be had. Just because we've done things a certain way for decades, doesn't mean that they need to stay that way.

Bottleneck

It's great to see how many companies are paying attention to Mental and Physical Health in the workplace. The movement is gaining momentum.

Yet, is everyone seeing themselves on the same playing field?

The challenge with the pyramid style of management, is that corporate rank also tends to come with a varying set of rules. This hierarchy has been in place for so long, that we don't even think about it.

For example, it is typically said that you move UP into management. You don't move laterally, or down. The organizational structure is most often a pyramid that starts small at the top, and broadens as it moves downwards towards as collars go from white to blue.

This perceived rank is the perfect example of a Hero Culture environment. The corner office, the high floor, the prestige of your own bathroom…

Now some companies get sneaky on their websites and invert the pyramid, but I've never spoken with a company that has introduced their janitor first at the National conference.

This is its own can of worms, but don't worry, the janitorial staff will clean it up.

This perceived rank also has it's own challenges when it comes to mental health support though. Ben Burdette – Lieutenant-Colonel, US AIR FORCE is an amazing man, father, husband and friend of mine. We recently had a great chat about the stress and anxiety that comes with rank in the military.

The pressure that comes with being the one to make the right call at precisely the right moment, when lives are at stake is some of the greatest pressure I could ever imagine. When all eyes are on you to decide whether people live or die, or at least to put your own people at risk is something that thankfully, very few of use have to concern ourselves with.

The thing with a move up rank is, that you are expected to ALWAYS have the right answer. This happens across corporations around the world all the time, however with much less drastic implications.

With all the money being spent on mental health support, very few executives are actually utilizing these newly promoted benefits for themselves. It's not that there is a scarce supply, they're available to everyone.

It has to do with the Hero Culture implications of CEO's showing vulnerability.

Again, this doesn't apply in all cases, but for the majority, the uptake on mental health support for executives falls short due to their perceived responsibility of being at the top and showing strength.

There are many top-level executives who are working more hours than they ever did. They have taken on the burden of having to perform, and feel that showing vulnerability, although they are encouraging this with their teams, it isn't appropriate for them. It's how they were taught... Be the hero, don't show weakness.

In addition to them foregoing their own health, those who look up to them are inclined to act the same way, as are the next, and the next and the next.

We need to continue to have the same conversations that we are having, but increase the level of engagement and support... on the high floor, in the corner office.

Account-Able

One of the best books that we've read with our kids is called 'Have you filled a bucket today' by: Carol McCloud. It's so important to us that in the kids' hallway, we have a sign that says "I will fill someone's bucket today".

You can be a bucket filler, or a bucket dipper, and it's all about your own happiness and the way we treat others. When you fill someone's bucket by doing something good and making them feel nice, you fill your own bucket too. The opposite is also true.

The following is an incredible share by Ben Burdette (who I mentioned in the last chapter), and it is, in my opinion, the perfect way to think about this concept from an adult lens. Thank you so much for sharing Ben.

"Mental health is hard. It's just that simple. We think we have a handle on it, then it slips through the cracks and we lose, or come close to losing a loved one, or a member of our team.

My biggest frustration when it comes to power, control and what I will call "chasing the flag", is that none of us started out that way. We were innocent, eager and in love with what we did. Better yet, we worked hard every day for the sake of doing something good. Sure, a bonus, advance in pay or even a bump in position were nice to have, but it was the glory of seeing something you did and having it be recognized.

But something changes in people. There is a point when one's true color is no longer hidden from everyone else. That moment where stress takes over, the job you have worked so hard for is on the line, the value and the energy you have poured into the uniform (in my case) goes away. And what is left is you. Only you. Your decisions, how you have treated others, the legacy you have left is all dependent on you and the choices you made.

Who you are as a human, matters. If you are genuine, it will show. If you are toxic, it will show. It may take time or the right event, but eventually your core will shine through, for good or bad. And it is at these moments when ones' true character is laid on a platter for all to see. When what someone really values doesn't match what they traded to achieve success, they may find themselves with a nice car and big house and no one to share it with.

This is when mental health finds its victims. It attacks them, screams lies at them, and tells them they are unworthy. Unfortunately, this also can happen when someone is too young, or when someone has segregated themselves from the world. Sadly, at these moments, for whatever reason, people find themselves hearing the voice that will consume them, often times making it is too much to bare.

I am truly blessed. I have an amazing hot wife and four beautiful kids (seriously....they are pretty awesome, and she is so hot). In almost 20 years of active-duty service and diving deep into the communities we called home, there is nothing that surprises us anymore. People will always be people and there is nothing we can do to change that.

But what we can change is how we respond. My wife has this amazing saying that permeates my mind every time a like scenario replays itself. As an example, she loves to tell our kids, "Your response......is your responsibility." I love this! So simple, yet so true. What we cannot control is others, but we do get a vote in how we respond. Just think about that…if we never had to have the last word, provided no response other than "we'd be glad to help," regardless of if it was our responsibility or not.

There is value in us all. We must find it, and help others find it too. It may not look the same to every person, but every person must not give up until they clearly understand that value. It is too fragile to live without and it could be the very thing that propels us, or destroys us and how we see the world."

Ben Burdette – Lieutenant-Colonel, US AIR FORCE
Louisiana, USA

The $10,000 Band-Aid

While we're on the topic, maybe it's time to think a little more about the problem and more importantly, the solution.

Recently, a major multi-national corporation made an announcement about a significant change to their health and wellness plan for their employees.

It was phenomenal! It's a huge step forward! They announced an increase in the benefit for mental health related support. For members of their group insurance coverage, each employee would now be eligible for up to $10,000 of reimbursement for mental heal support.

Wow! This is fantastic, and it truly is, but nobody stepped up and asked why their employees needed that much support. Now I'm not saying that that money should not be utilized, but it brings about the very pertinent question of wondering why do we need such a big band-aid.

This is but one example of many that reinforce the importance of this conversation. This comment is not to take away from the incredible thought behind this, but also knowing how health benefit work and the cost recovery built into these plans, the renewal will be significant if these benefits are used to their potential.

Pizza Over Everything

We're not there yet.

There is a huge pizza chain that is running commercials right now (at time of writing Feb 2023) with the slogan "Pizza over everything". Their most recent commercial depicts a pizza delivery driver who is en-route to bring delicious piping hot pizza to a beautiful family. When the driver approaches a fork in the road, the GPS recalculates, and rather than turning left down the bright, happy, flower filled road, the GPS says 'turn right to save 26 seconds'. This right turn appears to require him to pass through a hellish landscape full of fire and fear. The driver is obligated to turn right. This marginalizes the employee, puts them in danger, and reminds them that their value and physical safety is less, than the 26 seconds that will be saved in delivery time. We then see the happy family enjoying the pizza as the slogan appears "Pizza over everything".
Are You kidding me???

I thought we were getting better. I thought things were moving in the right direction.

Hero Culture is so deeply ingrained in our society, that a commercial like this is still able to make it to National television...

How many people had to sign off on this?

If I was the competing chain, I'd reproduce that commercial, but I'd have the driver turn left... My slogan would be "Can you wait 26 extra seconds? We're trying to keep our employees safe".

We've still got a long way to go.

Go Big To Give Big

Literally the day before I sent this book in for its final print copy review, I had a meeting with Randy Molland. We'd met a few times before, but it was on this day that I knew he had to be included in this project. He is a very special human who has a very simple, but specific mantra...

We believe in generosity being a core value of our lives, not just when it's convenient

We are not just givers once we have had success, we are givers all the time

Making impact is our passion and success is our motivation.

We play all out knowing that when
we **GO BIGGER**
We are able to **GIVE BIGGER**

We are the new generation of business owners...

His passion for humanity, for success, for living a full life is as inspiring as it gets. He lives a life with others' objectives first, but don't let that misdirect you from the focus he has on success and excellence.

Enjoy reading below, Randy's perspective on how to integrate and foster a philanthropic approach to business.

"Go Big to Give Big is a movement that is meant to inspire everyday humans to go bigger with their dreams and goals, so they can give bigger to the causes they believe in.

It all began when I heard a statement on a podcast that left me speechless: "If you want to make a million dollars a year, that's cool, just build your company to do two million and give a million dollars away, and don't feel bad about making your million dollars." The concept resonated with me deeply and came at a crucial time in my life.

At the time I was 28 years old, coming off the loss of one of my dear friends and starting a real estate investment company. I was fully immersed in the hustle culture and had just got out of the hospital after suffering a stress induced non-epileptic seizure... yes, I buried my pain with work and my body eventually just shut down.

While recovering I was feeling burnt out, exhausted and asking myself the question "what is all this for?"

Coincidentally, the day after asking myself that profound question, I heard that podcast quote. It hit me like a ton of bricks, providing the answer I had been seeking. There are many business owners like myself who become fixated on chasing the bottom line and money, losing sight of the beauty that surrounds entrepreneurship. Thankfully, at a young age, I recognized that money wasn't everything and that businesses can not only generate profits but can also make a meaningful impact.

This concept is not new, as exemplified by Tom's Shoes, a pioneer in the 1-for-1 model. They pledged to donate a pair of shoes to a person in need for every pair purchased. This is what we call a 'for-purpose' or 'socially responsible' business. This approach represents the convergence of capitalism and philanthropy, allowing entrepreneurs to use their capitalistic ways to solve philanthropic problems.

After realizing that I wanted to build a business that gave back, I started on the journey to find out what kind of charity I could support, how I could attach a giving component to my revenue, and what kind of impact I could make in the world. I was finally getting passionate about business again.

Within a few weeks I had taken our free meet-up and started charging $10 at the door as a donation. We took the 25 people that were showing up and started donating $250 a month to a local charity. Suddenly my burnout turned to excitement. And 25 people turned to 100 people and our $250 donation turned into a $1,000 monthly donation. I then figured out that I could apply the same principle to my real estate portfolio. I could donate $10 per door per month to charity.

My duplex started donating $20/month, my triplex started donating $30/month and so on and so on. Suddenly I was inspired to buy more real estate again and felt energetic and alive waking up every morning.

Then, one day, I turned to my business partner and said, "You know, the bigger we go, the more we can give. We just need to Go Big so we can Give Big!" That was the moment the movement was born and I realized that there was a better way of building businesses.

You see, so many people think that money will solve their problems or cover the pain we are in. But having more money won't solve the emptiness you feel inside. What I have come to realize though, is that if we use our money in the right way, we can actually buy ourselves more happiness and give ourselves a sense of purpose to enjoy the business we are building and avoid a lot of the burnout we feel just chasing money.

So I want to leave you with this. I challenge you to take something as simple as $10 a transaction and put it into a separate bank account and label that your "happiness account". Every quarter, use that money to do something good —donate to charity, provide blankets or food for the homeless, or help a struggling friend pay their rent. I promise, you will feel more driven and motivated to grow your business, hit new revenue milestones, and all because you will get addicted to the giving that is associated with it.

This is the new wave of entrepreneurship. It is the reason we must all strive to go big so that we can give big. By incorporating giving components into our businesses, we have the power to make a substantial impact on the world, support good causes and experience a profound sense of fulfillment, all while making the money we deserve."

Randy Molland – Founder, Go Big To Give Big
Victoria, BC Canada

Talkin 'Bout A Revolution

I get it... It's a lot, and it's complicated.

We have been living this way for generations, and Hero Culture is so deeply ingrained in our psyche. It affects our conversations. It affects our relationships. It affects our work and our self-worth.

Hero Culture affects everything we do.

We've taken this journey together this far, working through its definition, its cause, our addiction to chaos and crisis, how to tip time, the importance of resilience, and some specifics about where we've been when it comes to work.

Our job however is far from over. Time waits for nobody, so we continue through, with a keen awareness of the power of nothing, but we must also think about some factors already at play that will affect our future.

The revolution will continue. The conversations are happening. Our world is trying to figure it out. How are we going to accomplish such a monumental shift?

It's up to us which part of it we want to be involved in.

Disrupt or Be Disrupted

'Disrupt or be disrupted'. These 4 words were spoken to me by the CEO of a Global Finance company, and they've always stuck with me.

They are simple, elegant, and important. They come across different than the cliché 'the only constant is change'. They are a stark reminder of the competitive nature of the marketplace.

Considering what Hero Culture has done to our employment world and our lives, this lesson is truly more important than ever.

We discussed earlier about the short term financial costs associated with implementing changes to help us emerge, but we haven't yet taken the time to consider the long term threat to organizations who do not evolve their work environments.

There are progressive companies who are just as eager to win and take market share from your company as you felt when you were starting. Technology alone will not be sufficient for them to create market disruption.

**They need talent. They need people.
And they're coming after the best ones you got!**

And how are they going to persuade them? It's not with the Defined Benefit Pension plan that is facing longevity risk. It's not your ping pong table, a Cadillac, or a set of steak knives. It will be by rewarding them with a lifestyle that maximizes their ability to enjoy their life.

The benefits that will drive retention will not be the perks of the past. It's time to get working on this plan.

Disrupt or Be Disrupted!

On Purpose, For A Purpose

One of the most inspiring men that I have met over the past year, is Luke Askew. He is a father, a husband, and a visionary. He will be one of the great leaders of the upcoming generation and is wise beyond his years. These are some of his observations from his writing, "The purpose driven entrepreneur".

"Every successful idea starts as just a dream; a unique vision for the world, hidden on the inside of us, waiting for us to discover it and take responsibility for its fulfillment.

It was on the 15th of January 1929 a very powerful dream was born on the inside of a little baby boy by the name of Martin Luther King Jr. It would be a dream that would change the world and will be remembered for centuries.

For Dr. King, that dream was a world in which his four children would one day live in a nation where they would not be judged by the colour of their skin but by the content of their character.

In a time of great pain and sorrow, Dr. King discovered that the dream he carried would also be a light of hope for many & an opportunity to make a difference in the world. A dream that would go on to bring freedom to his people and put a stop to the injustice that was taking place.

He wasn't undertaking the project for financial gain, but for the purpose for which he had felt called to fulfill it.

Simply put, he was chosen before the foundations of the world to supply what the earth was demanding and so are you!

Within all of us is a unique vision of the world, concealed in the form of a dream that is continually knocking at the door of our hearts. A dream that when discovered will reveal to you the reason why you existed and the difference you were created to make.

The only reason why it has not yet come to pass is that it is waiting for you to accept the call and take responsibility for its fulfillment.

For me, my dream was discovered in a time of great pain. Feeling trapped working for pieces of paper rather than for a purpose, calling out for God to reveal to me the purpose in which he had created me for.

Seeing a generation so lost that they were choosing to kill themselves rather than letting go of the life they had created built on a lie. I felt the knocking and call to do something about it.

The trick is to see yourself as a new breed of purpose-driven leader; on a mission to fulfill the unique purpose that is calling you."

Luke Askew
Greater Manchester, England

Purpose x People x Process = Profit

How do we make more money? Ummmm... yeah, it's a valid question. Corporations need to be profitable. It's important.

I don't like to think of money as the goal. It's not a leading metric that predicts the future success of an organization. It is, however, a lagging metric that let's us know how we're doing. It doesn't have feelings, and it doesn't make one thing better that the other.

But it is crucial. Without money, without profit, the entity ceases to exist. We go bankrupt. If we are bankrupt, we cannot operate, and we cannot change the world.

Shareholder value is not to be overlooked. It can be easy to look at Corporate decisions and make claims that 'they're just doing this to look good in the paper and to increase shareholder value'. Well, guess what? THAT'S WHAT THEY'RE SUPPOSED TO DO.

The company needs to turn a profit to stay in business. Profit is not the part that makes a corporation seem evil to some, it's how we got there that matters.

Being a good Corporate Citizen is important. We only have one planet to nurture. The Corporate responsibility to our planet and to the humans on it is something that is improving... slowly.

I believe, however, that the value that we place on our investment in people, is lagging. Hero Culture promotes that people are a disposable commodity. The labour pool is large. Technology is reducing our need for human capital. If you don't like it, go find somewhere else to work...

This threat is losing its effectiveness. People are leaving their employers, in exchange for a better life, in record numbers.

> "We're not gonna take it.
> No, we ain't gonna take it.
> We're not gonna take it anymore.
>
> We've got the right to choose, and
> There ain't no way we'll lose it.
> This is our life, this is our song.
>
> We'll fight the powers that be, just
> Don't pick on our destiny, 'cause
> You don't know us, you don't belong.
>
> We're not gonna take it.
> No, we ain't gonna take it.
> We're not gonna take it anymore."
>
> -Twisted Sister - 1984

Let's review the formula:

Purpose x People x Process = Profit

What is important to note, is that this is a multiplication formula. Most times that we observe this, its shown as addition.

Small differentiation, but with huge implications. Each of the above factors has a significant multiplier impact on the end result.

In addition, People used to equate more directly to labour. With dramatic shifts in technology, the need for skilled human capital is continually on the rise. It's not that we just need people, we need specific people.

Labour is also very expensive, and with operating costs increasing so significantly, the investment in quality human capital is getting more difficult. At time of writing, we are seeing significant global layoffs as corporations pivot to maintain returns to shareholders.

This short-term-bias behaviour is significantly hindering the potential for long term profits. And when we hinder long term profit, we risk extinction. Again, the discussion is not simple, but those organizations who truly understand the importance of this will take the time to consider the long-term outcomes of short-term decisions, and understand the importance of the investment needed in their human capital, and the importance of eradicating Hero Culture from their organizations.

Balance Is Bullshit

Mike Cameron changed my thinking. He and I met, and instantly connected. One of the conversations that we had, was about work/life balance. So many people say it without thinking about it. Guess what? It's WRONG.

Mike has affected me in many ways, but this lesson about work/life integration, instead of balance has had a dramatic impact on my life. He has been one of the Humans who has been a great leader in the eradication of Hero Culture.

Here is the explanation in his words…

"OK, so I feel like I need to put in a little disclaimer here. It is important to note that this article is written by a man whose staff gave him the book "Workoholics: The Respectable Addicts" for Christmas some 5 or 6 years ago. It is also worth noting that I never did read the book. I will however say that I believe I have come a long way since then in my journey to 'becoming'. I want to share some of the insights I have had over the last several years and how I continue to work toward a life of fulfillment. This area is a constant work in progress for me and certainly not a destination that I believe one arrives at. We have to be ever vigilant of our mindset and ways of thinking in our quest to find alignment with our inner selves.

We hear the term "balance" thrown around a lot. We are told that we need to "find balance". We need to strive to have that perfect Work/Life balance. I'm here to tell you that that is a bunch of bullshit! Don't believe me? Let's look at the definition of the term that we throw around as gospel every day.

Balance: a condition in which different elements are equal or in the correct proportions.

I'm certain we can all agree that 'work' and 'life' are not elements that we want in equality. That leads us the conclusion that we must strive to have them in the correct proportions. Sounds reasonable. The trouble is, you cannot look at proportionate distribution without first quantifying each piece. Time is the most frequent measure we would use in this scenario. Traditional wisdom might suggest that a 'balanced life' is one where we spend 8 hours a day at work from Monday to Friday and the rest of the time in "life", whatever the heck that means.

My masculine, analytical, A-type brain wants to take this further and look at other areas of my life. What is the correct proportion of 'Me time'? What is the correct proportion of 'Family time'? What is the correct proportion of 'Fitness time'? You get the idea. If time is in act the correct unit of measure than really it should be as simple as defining the appropriate amount of hours for each 'segment' and having the discipline to stick to it. Unfortunately that is not really the way that life tends to work. There are a couple of inherent flaws with this model.

Is time really the appropriate measure? How do we accurately quantify it?

Do we measure the time that we are physically in our 'work' environment? Our home environment? What if our mind starts drifting at work to the football game we are going to go watch our son play that evening? What happens when we start thinking, or perhaps even stressing over, that project back at the office while we are at the ball game or out on date night with our spouse?

The idea that we have to have the correct proportion of each aspect of our life also pre-supposes that we live each of these segments in silos. That we can compartmentalize each of these items. The reality is usually quite a bit different. All of the areas of our life tend to cross over each other.

Our work life spills into our home life and vice versa. Let's face it, if we are having a really shitty day at the office it is not realistic to expect that as soon as you walk in that door to your home you can drop the burden of work that you are carrying and simply leave it outside ready to be picked up on your departure the next morning. The same holds true if you are having stresses in your life outside of work. When you walk through that office door there is no realistic way you can shed all of the financial anxiety those $15,000 orthodontics are causing you.

So what is the answer? As with most things in life I think you will find there is no magic answer. No one-size fits all remedy that will miraculously make everything OK. I do however, know that the answer lies in there somewhere. It starts with awareness and asking the question. If we don't ask the question we will never find the answers.

G.I. Gurdjieff was a Greek-Armenian philosopher that introduced a system of self-development called "The Fourth Way". He says something to the effect that "If you do not know you are in prison, escape is impossible."

The 'Fourth Way' to which the title refers is a method of inner development – "the way of the sly man," as Gurdjieff described it. This way is to be followed under the ordinary conditions of everyday life, as opposed from the three traditional ways that call for retirement from the world: those of the fakir, the monk, and the yogi, which Gurdjieff maintained could only result in partial, unbalanced development of man's potential.

For me part of the answer is to change the language I use. Instead of striving for "Balance", finding correct proportionate distribution of the components of my life, I have started to look for "Integration". In other words how do I successfully blend the components of my life to provide fulfillment and purpose. Let's look at the definition.

Integration [in-ti-grey-shuh n]
Noun: an act or instance of combining into an integral whole.

Boom! This makes so much more sense. My objective now does not become to have the 'right' proportional amounts of each component of my life but rather to find a way to combine all the elements into an 'integral whole'. This means that there is not a magic formula that you can apply to find that perfect mix of your parts. What it does mean, is that you need to find a way to combine each piece. Now, with practice you will start to find ways to implement integration into your life. When we talk in the context of work and home this means that you and your partner will both need to be on board with this concept. If one of you is looking for balance it will be difficult for the other to find integration.

If our partner expects us to be able to immediately toggle from "work mode" to "home mode" that becomes problematic. When you communicate well and both recognize that this is not an easily achievable concept, then together you can start to find ways to integrate that transition time into your life. Make this practice intentional. Make it a bonding experience.

For me the practice of yoga has been a great analogy and

therefore practice of some of these concepts. In yoga the transitions between poses are especially important. They are times where we practice moving from one pose to the next, maintaining our rhythm of breathing, staying present in those moments 'in between'. If we only focus on mastering the poses, or the 'activities' in life then we create this rushed, jerky, uncomfortable life where we simply jump from one test to the next. We need to slow down, breath and stop to smell the roses so to speak.

When I think of balance it puts a complete emphasis on the 'pieces' and doesn't really allow us to focus on, or practice the transition with the objective of achieving that integral whole.
By shifting focus from balance to integration we are allowed to slow down, enjoy the in between and focus on creating those seamless transitions between the multiple facets of our life.

So my question for you is "Where can you find better integration in your life?"

- Mike Cameron - Speaker, Author, Human
www.mikecameron.ca - Canmore, AB, Canada

Leveraging Technology

How do you write an authentic section about leveraging technology?

You get and AI Chat bot to write it for you... P.S. - This chapter took 24 seconds to create/

Me: write 750 words on the power of AI and its role in the businesses of the future. Describe how AI will reduce mundane tasks, increase efficiency, and improve quality of life for employees.

Chat GPT: Artificial intelligence (AI) has been rapidly changing the way we live and work. In recent years, its impact has been felt in a variety of industries, from healthcare and finance to retail and transportation. As AI technology continues to advance, its influence on businesses is expected to only become more pronounced. In this article, we will examine the power of AI and its role in the businesses of the future.

One of the key benefits of AI is its ability to reduce mundane tasks. Many of the repetitive, time-consuming tasks that employees currently perform can be automated using AI. This not only saves employees time, but also reduces the risk of human error, freeing them up to focus on more important, strategic work. For example, AI can be used to automate the process of data entry, freeing up employees to focus on analyzing and making use of that data.

Another way in which AI is expected to benefit businesses is by increasing efficiency. AI algorithms can analyze large amounts of data and identify patterns and relationships much faster than a human could. This enables businesses to make more informed decisions, identify opportunities for improvement, and optimize their processes. For example, AI can be used to analyze sales data to identify which products are selling well and which are not, allowing businesses to make more informed decisions about which products to stock and promote.

In addition to improving efficiency, AI is also expected to improve the quality of life for employees. For example, AI-powered chatbots can handle simple customer service inquiries, freeing up employees to focus on more complex tasks. Additionally, AI can be used to automate routine administrative tasks, such as scheduling and email management, freeing up time for employees to focus on more important tasks.

The potential of AI to transform businesses is not limited to the improvement of efficiency and quality of life for employees. AI can also help businesses stay ahead of the competition by providing them with a competitive advantage.

For example, businesses that are able to harness the power of AI to analyze large amounts of data and identify trends and patterns will have a significant advantage over those that do not. Additionally, businesses that are able to automate routine tasks using AI will be able to operate more efficiently, reducing costs and increasing profits.

One of the most exciting aspects of AI is its potential to create new business opportunities. As AI technology continues to advance, it is likely that new applications and uses will emerge. For example, AI can be used to develop new products and services, such as personalized recommendations or predictive analytics. Additionally, AI can be used to create new business models, such as on-demand services or subscription-based offerings.

Despite the many benefits of AI, there are also some potential risks and challenges that businesses will need to be aware of. For example, there is a risk that AI will lead to job displacement, as some jobs are automated and replaced by machines. This is a concern for many employees, who may fear that their jobs will become obsolete in the future. Additionally, there is a risk that AI algorithms may perpetuate biases and discrimination, leading to unfair outcomes for some individuals and groups.

Another challenge that businesses will face as they adopt AI is the need for investment in new technology and training for employees. Implementing AI technology can be expensive, and businesses will need to ensure that they have the resources and expertise necessary to successfully integrate AI into their operations. Additionally, employees will need to be trained on how to use AI, as well as how to work with AI- powered systems and technologies.

Despite these challenges, the potential benefits of AI are likely to far outweigh the risks and challenges in the long run. As AI technology continues to advance, businesses that are able to successfully adopt and integrate AI into their operations will have a significant advantage over those that do not.

Source: https://chat.openai.com/chat

To Attract You Must Be Attractive

Whether you are a Multi-National Corporation wanting to attract key human capital, or a Sole Proprietor looking to sell your business, in order to attract, you must be attractive.

I was speaking with a very good friend and former colleague recently. He and I both had been working for the same company in the past, and both departed around the same time. We were speaking about a Used Car lot in a small town that he was considering purchasing to add to his business portfolio. Choosing a new way of life compared to the Hero he had portrayed for decades.

He had done his research. He had visions of on-line sales, AI chat support, e-financing and pre-approvals, and an inventory system designed to cross-sell vehicles from other small dealerships in the region. It was a brilliant and revolutionary concept compared to the way that the business was currently being run.

The existing owner, who had been running the lot for 35 years, explained to him, all the reasons why his new fancy idea would never work. "Just run it how I've been doing for 35 years..." He talked himself right out of the sale, and likely had some sharp commentary about 'kids' these days... The thing that we need to pay attention to here is that in order to attract, we must be attractive.

In the Financial Services industry, in which I have spent the greatest amount of time out of my entire professional career, there are businesses of enormous size being run by Financial Advisors, many of whom are looking to pass their legacy down to their children in the coming years.

They toiled away for decades to build an empire, intended to support their family for generations to come. They are also some of the most susceptible to mental and physical illness. Their business is their identity. Many of them, still addicted to Hero Culture and 'being busy to be successful', feel that they are unable to retire. What will they be without their business? This identity crisis is causing too many in the boomer generation to crash and suffer significantly when they sell their businesses, or retire. Quite often, they're afraid to retire, because they fear for what will remain of their identity.

They made significant sacrifices throughout their lives, by working, instead of attending their kids sporting events. They traded their marital bliss, their physical health and mental strength, all in the name of being the hero.

Here's the thing... Many of the children have NO INTEREST whatsoever in getting into Mom or Dad's business. We'll discuss the reason why, and it will uncover the story behind creating a business that is attractive to the upcoming generation by exploring this from an alternative lens.

Your kids feel guilty and don't know how to tell you...

I have been asked by several millennial adults to please help them explain to their parents why they don't want to go into the family business and/or live life the same way.

They feel guilty, and don't want to disappoint you, and they don't know how to talk to you about it.

If you have children who you are grooming to take over the family business, please take some time and sit down with them and have a real heart-to-heart. Ask them questions and listen to what they have to say. You are concerned about their future and their ability to financially thrive in this changing world, and they are worried about your health. They want to make sure that you'll be around to play with the grandkids.
It's really hard for them to bring this up, but so many of them that I have spoken with, really want to talk about this, but they don't want to upset you.

Consider this a PSA, on behalf of the Millennials.

Your kids love you so much. Even though there were times that you were not around, they know you love them. They are grateful for the vacations, or the cottage, and for everything that you sacrificed for them. This however burdens them with guilt, as they don't want to disappoint you, by letting you know that they don't want to live the same way that you did. The reason is, they don't want to develop the same health and relationship problems.

More so, they wish that you didn't have them. They just want their Mom and Dad to be happy and to enjoy a beautiful life, even if it means giving up the cottage.

The generation that you are grooming to take senior leadership roles, or to take over your business are incredibly intelligent. How could they not be, they had you as their parents and leaders.

But every generation helps evolve our society, and they have seen the impact that working too hard, without dealing with the emotional side of things, has had on the mental and physical health of your generation.

They have also grown up in the digital age. Knowledge is not as important to them as it is to you, because knowledge is available on- demand now.

I remember hearing an analogy about the Borg, who were antagonists in the Star Trek series. They had infinite knowledge, which at the time, was unheard of. Currently, we do not have the chips implanted in us, but the infinite knowledge machine is in everyone's pockets at all times.

To a certain extent, we have already become the Borg.

They also value the time in between starting work at 20 and retiring at 65, and they're not willing to trade it for money. In Tim Ferris' iconic book the 4-hour-work-week, he suggests to us that we should live life as a series of mini retirements, and he isn't wrong.

There is a ton of content here, and we should bring it to a close soon, so to bring this all together, we need to take everything in the book until now, and really think about the businesses that we are running. Whether they be a multi-national corporation or a sole-proprietor business, for us to attract, we must be attractive.

And also, don't forget to go talk to your kids...

Glamorizing Exhaustion

Closer to the time of writing this book, was when I had the pleasure of meeting and becoming friends with Lorna Wilkins, Co-Founder–Tommy Hatto Online. Lorna, like so many other Millennials, is part of the movement that is creating our new world.

Her perspective on living life, rather than trudging through it and racing to the finish is inspiring. She is creating a world that will support being Human over pretending to be a Hero.

In her own words, she shares a personal perspective that is shared by the majority of her fellow Millennials, and whom like her, are becoming the future leaders and agents of change.

"Working long hours, taking minimal breaks and prioritizing work over relationships is the key to success – that's what society tells you, and what I believed for a very long time.

Having watched my father work long hours when growing up, it seemed only right to follow his example if I were to achieve my full potential. At one point in my early working years, I would start my translation work at 4am, go to my day job at 9am and on finishing at 5pm, would then return home and continue translating until 11pm. This became my daily routine, so it's no surprise that I caused myself to burn out and experience severe anxiety and depression from the amount of pressure that I had put myself under just to 'succeed'.

Of course, I had perpetuated most of this pressure myself, based on the expectation of who I had to be. I was lucky that my parents supported my decision in whatever path I wanted to follow, yet even so, I was still afraid to tell them that I wanted to give up my translation career because it was destroying my mental health. The guilt I felt was huge. They had supported me through University and helped fund my internship, so the thought of telling them that I wanted to walk away terrified me. Money didn't matter, but my time and quality of life did.

Myself and other millennials have witnessed the impact that our parents' generation had. We learn from our parents, so their habits affect us. As a parent, it's important to demonstrate the importance of balancing hard work with both physical and mental wellbeing.

This toxic work culture, which has been so normalised, needs to change. Across social media, this way of working is still very much glamourized and so the pressure that young people feel is ever-growing.

This was one of my main driving forces for wanting to leave the corporate world and support businesses in driving change in the workplace through applying a human approach.

Millennials and Gen Z are the future of the workforce and value their wellbeing. Not only do they want flexibility and to be heard, but they also want work to fit around their lifestyle rather than the other way round. This is why businesses need to act now to adopt this new way of working if they want to stay ahead.

My generation and those following on want to enjoy a successful career that also allows us to invest in those things that bring us joy, and to spend time with the people most important in our lives. In this way, we all become enriched."

Lorna Wilkins – Co-Founder, Tommy Hatto Online
Swindon, England.

Competence

Giselle Saati is one of the most resilient women that I have had the pleasure of getting to know along this journey. Spend 5 minutes with her and you will quickly realize that you are in the presence of a formidable Human.

Her humility, combined with her passion for the Human journey, welcomes you immediately.

Her contribution below only begins to scratch the surface of the deep understanding that she has on Human performance.

Her words that follow, help us understand the importance of stress in our evolving world.

"Work-life-balance is a hot topic these days as employers are mandating their employees to return to the office. Trying to understand the oscillation between recovery and stress is still too difficult to understand or implement in a highly competitive and individualistic world.

Work or stress is a necessity in life. We need it to grow. But how much stress is too much? And more importantly, what type of stress should we undertake? For instance, engaging in a rigorous, physical activity in the gym for muscle development or to improve physical fitness, is in and of itself a "good" stress.

Now let's add another variable to the equation, length of time. A three-hour workout may be excessive or "bad" for a beginner or intermediate individual, but for a professional athlete that may be standard. By adding more variables such as temperament, personality, history, emotional pattern; we make this equation incredibly complex and make it exceedingly more difficult to find "balance".

Typically, we see stress as isolated, one-time events, such as a car accidents, the death of a loved one, a relationship breakup, etc. But there are other stresses that are subtle, silent, and chronic, like a dripping faucet. For instance, the suppression of emotions, extreme stoicism, emotional deprivation, silently putting up with discomfort, or even role reversals between parent and child. Dr. Gabor Maté, a renowned expert in addiction, stress, and childhood development, has dedicated an entire book about these subtle stresses and the impacts it can have on our bodies and the quality of living. He provides several case studies of how our closest relationships play a major role on our biological state.

> **"Psychological influences make a decisive biological contribution to the onset of malignant disease through the interconnections linking the components of the body's stress apparatus: the nerves, the hormonal glands, the immune system and he brain centres where emotions are perceived and processed."**
> Maté, D. (2003). When the Body Says No

As a first generation Canadian, I've experienced first-hand the responsibility and pressure that comes with being raised by parents who've escaped a war-torn country. The demands that I've put on myself to "succeed" was a subtle stress that went undetected. Till this day, I say to myself "I need to be stronger, better faster." Although my parents have provided me with opportunities and financial needs, they were not able to meet my emotional needs. I have devoted a considerable amount of time and energy to becoming physically and mentally strong, only to compensate for the fear of being perceived weak and being abandoned. It wasn't until much later in my life that these fears and stresses started manifesting physically. Had they not been addressed, through therapy, I might have increased the probability of developing a disease such as Cancer, Alzheimer's, Arthritis, etc.

There are many people, who share my story and part of my practice involves helping people build emotional competence. Which involves learning who you are and be able to have relationships with others in a non-victimized, non-self- harming way."

Giselle Saati – CEO GS Fortitude
Toronto - Canada

The Sacred Hierarchy

This may be the most important triangle that I've ever made, and it ties so many things that we are talking about, together into a super powerful place. We have explored the concept of tipping time, and harnessing the power of nothing, along with a multitude of other topics, but it is the Sacred Hierarchy that has the ability to bring us to a deeper place of contentment.

The most famous, and generally accepted Hierarchy of Human Needs was defined by Abraham Maslow in his 1943 paper "A Theory of Human Motivation". Maslow broke his hierarchy into deficiency and growth needs, but this distinction is rarely discussed in a Hero Culture life. We have grown to group and define his entire pyramid as a prerequisite for being a human hero.

It is for this reason that I believe that it is necessary to simplify and to create a simplified hierarchy of human needs.

Let's discuss first how Maslow's hierarchy can be misleading. I am in full agreement with the first two layers of Physiological and safety & security needs. To live a life of contentment, in our modern day society, it is imperative to have food, water, shelter and to be free from the threat of physical danger.

Where I start to vary is when we move beyond these base levels. The suggestion of a need for belonging and love, esteem, self-actualization and transcendence, reinforces our Hero Culture mindset, suggesting that the lack of achievement of these levels makes us incomplete as humans.

In place of these needs, I propose that we adopt a top tier level of human needs to be defined as self-acceptance. This allows us to avoid the trap of seeking these traditional higher level wants as mandatory, leaving us unfulfilled.

Now the journey to self-acceptance may be a road filled with twists and turns, and it may take us continued work to achieve it, but with the understanding of tipping time, combined with the ability to harness the power of nothing, we may be able to understand how much easier it actually is to get there.

If you have a clear grasp of the concept that although all the events in our life touch one another, they are not connected, and that the power to achieve everything you've ever desired exists continually in the present moment, self-acceptance becomes much less of a daunting task.

This brings calm and contentment into our lives with greater ease, and further sets us apart from the former addiction that we had for chaos and crisis.

Now, this does not negate the opportunity for us to further pursue the higher levels of Maslow's original pyramid, in fact it does the opposite. By integrating the Sacred Hierarchy into our lives, and operating from a state of self-acceptance, it makes the achievement of these higher states more easily achievable, should you choose to pursue them.

CHO - Chief Heart Officer

One of the best parts of studying Hero Culture, has been meeting amazing people around the globe who also believe that there is a better way for us to do things. The more people you meet, the more you realize that you are not alone in your beliefs and dreams of an evolving structure.

One of those amazing Humans is Sandra Crouzet, who lives in Zurich, Switzerland. We plan to ski together when we can, but for now we share our passion for a better work experience. Her track record is exemplary, but it is her passion for humanizing the workforce through the growth of the C-Suite with the addition of the CHO or Chief Heart Officer Role is even a greater example of what an amazing human she is.

She explains it best in her words that follow here.

"Let's be clear, we are here to do business but let's do it HUMAN! Selling our products and services and focusing on hopefully sustainable growth is a goal all organizations have.

So, when I talk about employing a Chief Heart Officer this has not to do with pampering your people and being scared of setting expectations and securing that ambitious business goals are met.

When I recommend to organizations to employ a Chief Heart Officer, it's because we should be focused on doing business in a sustainable and human way, ensuring that our most important asset, our people, remain healthy, dedicated, motivated, and engaged with the organization.

We need to be surrounded by the right environment – an environment of trust, the right culture, the psychological and emotional safety that enables us to become the best version of ourselves, a surrounding where we are not being judged but our strengths are recognized and used in the favor of the people and the organizations' goal achievements, an environment where we can speak up and that enables us to be seen, heard and valued.

There is no one size fits all. Human beings all have different and unique personalities. Through people centric leadership with a strong individual focus, interest and curiosity of the person sitting opposite and an open-minded approach we can identify the unique skills each person adds and the necessary environment the person needs to perform at their best level in order to achieve ambitious business goals.

**Only if we treat adults as adults,
will they behave like adults.**

The Chief Heart Officer role plays an important part in securing that a culture of trust is created, implemented, and lived top down.

We are not talking a beautiful text in strategic papers, we are talking a person that always has an open door, that is approachable, that leads with the heart and that works for the people of the organization rather than the other way around. We are talking about a servant leader.

The CHO holds the following responsibilities:
- Employees are the company's internal customers, and the Chief Heart Officer is responsible to identify what their employees need and respond accordingly. It's also
- essential that they're able to coach and drive individuals toward their own personal objectives while inspiring and leading them through change . Is a creator of multiple
- awesome business and people- oriented practices. Is in charge of the well-being and overall pleasure of the
- company's personnel. Brings out a desire for happiness in the workplace and a pleasant employee experience.
- Ensures that employees know they are valued, becoming more efficient and productive. Knows the practical and
- motivating aspects of every employee they handle. A Chief Heart Officer is someone who has a grasp on the
- company's employees' hearts and minds. Is the right hand to the CEO and connects heart & hustle
-
-

- Is in touch with the heartbeat of every single person in the organization and lives "people first" value. Is a servant
- leader and works for the people rather than the people working for CHO. Lives their purpose. Is a mentor with
- view on mentorship: connection, trust and empathy.
- Creates longevity and loyalty. Taking care of employees' wellness and wellbeing and ensures employees are happy
- turning up to work. Has one-on-one meetings. Talking and resolving issues. Fosters a culture of trust and
- collaboration, helping teams to move to the next level of
- company's success in all areas. Helps people to work in a healthy work environment and through this people are
- more likely to stay – reducing turnover and its related cost. Ensures that employees become fans of the organization. Continually works on the advancement of company
- culture.
-

What is in it for the organization when employing a Chief Heart Officer

- Employees feel looked after and cared for – enabling people to feel secure, respected valued and happy.
- Trust culture is created as a basis for authentic KPI measures.

- Provides an emotionally & psychologically safe environment. Skill set optimization and potential
- identification - Providing education and training to obtain and boost the essential skills of all employees. Moves the right potential into the right roles - creating an organization
- of top performers. Supports leaders in developing people centric leadership. Makes developments tangible and fact
- based, through people analytics. Reduces turnover
- Increases efficiency – running independent and effective teams Increases engagement Increases motivation Enhances
- transparent and authentic communication
-

-
-
-

Companies must understand the power of improving employee well-being. Content and satisfied employees will reduce turnover, which can be cost-effective for the organization.

So let's create WIN-WIN situations for our people because they will be happy and healthy and for the organization as it will achieve ambitious business results through highly motivated, engaged and efficient employees."

Sandra Crouzet, CHO – Chief Heart Officer
Zurich, Switzerland

Drive Safe

Ever since I was 16 years old, every time I was about to leave the house, my Mom would say to me "Drive Safe." "Yes mom" I'd reply. 30 years later, whenever I go visit my parents, every time I am about to leave the house, it's still the same.
But let's be honest, did we always drive safe?

The same thing happens for us in Hero Culture. We believe that we have a handle on things. We push it and push it, and do our best to stay between the lines, but think that we can shave off a few seconds here and there. It's like seeing the GPS arrival time as a challenge. We think that we can get there sooner.

In the airplane safety briefing, what do we hear? "Always put on your mask before assisting others". But what would we actually do? Let's hope we don't have to find out.

Let's bring back the quote from Simone Biles:

> **"We have to protect our minds and our bodies and not just go out and do what the world wants us to do".**

Wear your seatbelt, don't speed, drink in moderation, do moderation in moderation... but what about Crisis, what about our friend Chaos?

We live lives where we crave smashing into the wall at 500 MPH before we make a change.

In the coaching world, business conversations tend to blend into personal, marital and relationship conversations.

Because if we're not happy at home it spills into work. It's that whole work/life integration part that Mike Cameron talked about earlier.

And it's not a joke. If we don't deal with our demons when they are small, they will conquer us in the end. Don't let them grow.

Go to therapy, talk to co-workers, talk to your boss, talk to God, talk to yourself.

This part of our lives seems to be gaining acceptance, and it is a crucial part to leaving the Hero where they belong, and just be human.

This pattern that we've been following really needs to change, and it begins with us!

Continuation

It's Enough To Be Human...

We've just gone through one heck of a journey. Thank you for giving yourself the time and permission to take in the content.

We opened this conversation with the topic of 'Just Be Yourself'. It really should be that simple, shouldn't it...

Well, the thing about being Human, is that it is complicated, and there isn't just one solution. The answer to almost every question in life is, it depends. We're all just making it up as we go along.

The beautiful part of the human journey is the uniqueness in which we all experience the world. Somewhere along the way, we all get lost, and almost always, we all get found. Our timelines are unique, and our experiences personal.

For too many decades, we have lived the Hero's Journey, when what we were supposed to do was live the Human's Journey. The former is intended simply to teach us lessons, and we never should have allowed it to take over our lives.

The great news is, we have a choice. We have a choice to consider how we've been living. We have a choice to decide whether that way should change for us. We have a choice to live the life that we want... All we have to do is choose it.

In the process of writing this book, I joined 32 Authors from around the globe, who were all on the same journey of getting their scripts done in a week. It was truly magical. On the 5th day of writing, I went skiing instead of continuing writing. Living in the mountains, we are fortunate to be able to strap on our boards at the front door and just go.

One of the authors made a comment, that was truly supportive and in appreciation of the life we chose for our family, stated "I want Derek's life". It was appreciative and supportive, but the truth is, I get that a lot. The mountains are beautiful and not for once do I take it for granted, but the secret to living here is simple, just come live here. And if you don't love the snow, go somewhere that brings you the most happiness.

In our modern day society, we all have the freedom to choose the life that we want. Our circumstances all vary, but the choice to choose lives within us, regardless of our conditions.

The thing is, everything is a trade-off. What we are seeking, what we desire, what we believe. It's all a choice, and every action we make is a trade of an alternate opportunity.

I believe that identifying Hero Culture is of significant value to understanding how we got to where we're at in society, and that it unlocks the opportunity to escape it.

We don't need to upheave our lives, and make dramatic shifts unless we choose to. Living with the understanding of the power of nothing, allows you to tip time, as frequently as you'd like, heck even constantly. The power of nothing provides us quiet, and in a moment of quiet, when the past and future are disconnected, our freedom becomes infinite.

I urge you to consider the trade of chaos and crisis for the calm of quiet contentment. Choose resilience over courage.

Bring these ideas forward. Don't simply take that the way it is, is the way it is. If you desire a change in your life, don't wait until you hit the wall. Apply the brakes now, get out and take a walk around.

This world is full of abundance, go forth an seek it.

It's enough to be human, it's always been enough.

Thank You.

Every Day Human

Left to right: Kai Scott, President: TransFocus. Dr Tanya Gee, Doctor of Traditional Chinese Medicine. Derek Strokon, Founder: Every Day Human and Sacred Line Consulting

So where do we go from here?

There is no Conclusion to this book, only a Continuation. Simply becoming aware of our surroundings and the significant impact that Hero Culture has had on our Human Journey is not enough.

Change, as we discussed is a complex problem. The quantum entanglement of moving forward means that with each piece affecting another, one step forward may feel like a step backwards, and conversely, sometimes backwards must occur first.

Our emergence from Hero Culture is not going to happen all at once. We must expand our commitment to continuing the conversation and improving our understanding of the issues at hand.

Our mission will advance, one person, and one step at a time. The devotion to continual improvement and making specific, intentional change is important.

For this reason, I started Every Day Human. In this space our focus is to create a community for those who are passionate about emerging from the illusory grasp of Hero Culture.

If you would like to get involved. If you have a different perspective. If you feel that we need to speak to your organization... Please reach out.

www.everydayhuman.me

The Human's Journey

I wrote the following while I was working on my TEDx script and felt that it was appropriate to include. Is it the next book? Honestly who knows. Maybe the next book is called FLOW: Allowing Success to Catch You Rather Than Chasing It.

I'm leaving it here, raw and unedited, with no context. Make of it what you wish. I have not edited it, or adapted it to suit the content of the book you have just read. It is simply there if you wish to absorb it.

What if we imagined a new way? What if we redesigned the Hero's Journey, and structured it for a new way of living?

What if we didn't give Chaos and Crisis all the credit, and instead lived a life of contentment?

What if we used the Hero's Journey as it was intended, to teach us life lessons.?

What if we separated the Hero from the Human, and put the Hero back where they belong... On the Screen, in the Books and on Stage?

What if we truly believed that it is enough to be Human?

What if this was the way that we lived our lives and told stories?

What would it be like then?

The Human's Journey (Est. 2023)

1. Ordinary World – **Chaos and Crisis**

This is where the hero exists before their journey of contentment begins, oblivious of the adventures to come. It's where most of us are living right now, and it's relatable. It's a safe place, yet it is a place of uncontrolled compression and complacency, where we are taught that content = boring, and boring = bad. Seeking chaos and crisis, our hero is oblivious to the value of this place of contentment and is living in compression.

We are held here, seeing the outside world, seeking more, yet unable to act upon it.

We will return full circle to a different, awakened version of this same place.

2. Call To Adventure – **The Great Realization.**

This is where our hero begins to awaken. The realization is the discovery that change is not contingent on chaos or crisis.

Although it still may be the starting point, there is no need for a threat to personal safety, family, or way of life. It is simply the awakening that the traditional hero's journey has found itself too deeply ingrained in our society, and has overpowered our ability to change without crisis.

3. Refusal Of The Call – **Resilience over Courage**

Our hero must make the next step in realization. They are aware of courage. It's been ingrained throughout history. The ability to change starts to become a potential reality.

This moment of hesitation, which traditionally is defined as seeking courage is replaced with the development and establishment of resilience. This extends opportunity over time, rather than having to time it perfectly, or take a leap. Courage requires a moment or an opportunity, but resilience provides the ability to replace courage with conviction, passion with purpose, and bravado with bravery.

4. Meeting The Mentor –**Confronting Compression and Tipping Time**

The mentor is Tipping Time. The mentor is the self.

The effective part of this stage is where the Hero gains the knowledge that the catalyst to change is not an external factor. Crisis and Chaos are supposed to be the last straw, not the desired path. The way to move past the world of compression is to learn how to tip time, how to turn the hourglass sideways.

The hero must decide whether to break free from the world of compression, to see beyond the walls that they have constructed themselves. The world of compression is safe. It's comfortable.

Sometimes the compressed world has everything in it that the hero wants. The hero must self assess. What needs to stay, what needs to go?

5. Crossing The Threshold – **Designing the new normal.**

Designing the new normal. Our hero is now ready to begin their quest. Establishment of their non-negotiables begins here. What am I willing to live with, what am I unwilling to live without? What do I truly want my life to look like?

This is where growth and change become a reality and action starts to be taken.

6. Tests, Allies, Enemies – **Avoiding the pitfalls of Living your best life and changing the narrative**

Now in the process of change, the Hero begins to implement the strategies of change. The journey starts to become clearer.

They meet the allies - those who are in the process of changing for the right reason – those who are truly awake (and probably boring).

They meet the enemies - The posers - the 007's (IG Influencers), those 'living their best life', and people who are woke and changing the narrative.

They face the tests of returning to the old world, falling back into the comfortable life of uncontrolled compression.

The hero faces the test of resilience, conviction, purpose and bravery.

7. Reward (Seizing The Sword) – **Embracing Contentment**

After deciding to make the significant change and implementing the strategy for growth, the realization has created the opportunity for implementation. Although potentially triggered by a crisis event, it is clearly understood that the crisis would have been the last straw, not the requirement. The Hero is aware that change in the future is dependent on the continued development of the sacred and level of resilience that they possess.

The empowered Hero is now fully awake, and returns to create the life of contentment, understanding that contentment doesn't equal boring, and boring doesn't equal bad. Contentment = awakened, and awakened = good.

Opportunity is now boundless, and decisions on moving forward are made with clarity.

8. Return With The Elixir – **Invoking the Sigmoid Curve**

With boundless opportunity at their fingertips, the Hero continues to develop a life of contentment. Once awakened and clear on purpose and what is sacred, the Hero's resilience continues to strengthen. New challenges now have a defined direction and become more easily achievable.

Without the need for Chaos and Crisis, the world falls into alignment. Lifestyle design becomes a continued priority, and refinement of purpose continues.

Aware that growth happens at the bottom of the curve, the awakened Hero begins to focus on this based on a sigmoid curve rather than a sin wave.

The Hero returns to their origin state, awakened and forever changed.

Acknowledgements

Regardless of the name on the cover, a book is never written by a single person, and this book is no exception. Every word in this book has been influenced by every experience that I've gone through, and I'm grateful for every single one of them, even the soul-crushing, challenging ones, because its led me here.

Although this list is not exhaustive, there are some people that I would like to mention by name that have had a very significant impact on the writing of this book.

First and foremost to Tania Ehman, my writing and concept coach. Our path of discovery together forced us to take an honest look at Hero Culture, and led to the discovery of tipping time and birthed the journey that I am now on. This book is as much yours as it is mine. You challenged me to go so deep on this learning path, and I will always be forever grateful
To Wendy Leroux, my TEDx speaking coach, along with the entire team at TEDx Surrey, and my fellow speakers. Without your passion, support, encouragement, and expertise, I wouldn't have made it to the TEDx stage. That day in rehearsal that I forgot all my lines, and was about to run off stage, and never return, would not have turned out as it did without ALL of you. "Love You!!!"

Acknowledgements

In order that contributions were received - to: Kai Scott, Katy McFee, Greg Kettner, Ben Burdette, Luke Askew, Mike Cameron, Lorna Wilkins, Giselle Saati, Sandra Crouzet, and Randy Molland...

I count myself so lucky to have each of you in my lives. Having met you, from all around the world, is such a blessing. You all embody the spirit of Human Being Human, and I'm so grateful that you have shared your wisdom and perspective in these pages.

We all come from very different story lines, but the one that unites us is the passion we have for the Human journey. That is what makes us all truly Human. These pages would not be nearly as meaningful without your collaboration, and honesty.
Thank You!

To Mom and Dad... For your endless love and support, and for having made me into the man I am today. Your recent journey is the fuel that feeds my passion for sharing this message, but there's no way I would have ever gotten here without your guidance and belief in me.

To Jenn, Tristan and Amelia. You are my favourite Humans. You inspire me daily to continue to become a better man, husband and daddy. Thank you for believing in me and for all of you, staying real to yourselves.

About The Author

Derek is a keynote and TEDx speaker, and the #1 International Best-Selling Author of "Stop Stalling Start Selling". He is a Human Resilience Researchers, and Business Consultant, whose practice focuses on Purpose, People and Process Development and Implementation.

His award-winning approach to sales excellence is driven by a team-centered approach of 'Strength Through Vulnerability'. His relentless passion for evangelizing the 'Human Journey', is both inspiring and contagious.

Derek received a Bachelor of Arts in Economics from Simon Fraser University and is a Certified Professional Coach from World Coach Institute. Corporately recognized in 2018 as the National Sales Force Grow Leader, among many other accolades for sales excellence, he also attained his LLQP Full, MFDA, Labour Sponsored Fund and Branch Managers Course certifications.

About The Author

A seasoned Sales veteran with a Retail, Automotive, Food-Service and Financial Services background, Derek has led teams to success by igniting passion, simplifying solutions, and integrating processes.

He is the Founder of the Give Cancer The Finger Foundation, the Founder of Sacred Line Consulting, a Multi-National Coaching and Consulting firm, CEO of Polar Cold Caps Canada, and President of Every Day Human, which was borne out of the process of exploring this concept.

Derek spends the majority of his education development time, studying Resilience and Hero Culture, working on strategies to minimize the amount of time that life interferes with living.

Derek lives in Sun Peaks, BC, Canada, with his wife and 2 children. They love the outdoors, know what is sacred to them, and focus on lifestyle integration. His positive, essential approach is infectious, and always 100% authentic.

From 1:1 coaching, to large keynote addresses, you will be grateful for involving him to enhance your teams' success.

To engage Derek for keynotes, coaching or consulting projects, or to share a story of how this book helped you, reach out to him on any major social media platform, by e-mail at admin@sacredline.ca or toll free (877) 811-6553, or find his latest project at www.derekstrokon.com.

Notes

Notes

Notes

Notes

www.ingramcontent.com/pod-product-compliance
Lightning Source LLC
LaVergne TN
LVHW011824060526
838200LV00053B/3895